March 2019

To:
   Jimmy, Jeanne,
   Ana, and James

(Wayne and I love you
   very much!)

FINDING JOY

Blessings on your
journey of
"Finding Joy"
daily!
Joy C. Brown
Nehemiah 8:10

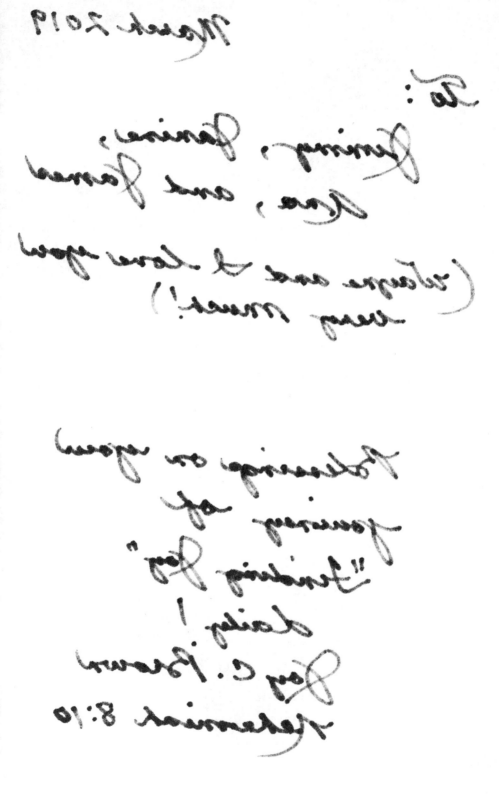

FINDING JOY

70 LIFE LESSONS
ALONG THE WAY

Joy C. Brown

XULON PRESS

Xulon Press
2301 Lucien Way #415
Maitland, FL 32751
407.339.4217
www.xulonpress.com

Printed in the United States of America.

ISBN-13: 9781545638330

DEDICATION

To my Facebook Friends,

Your friendship, encouragement, support, comments, and requests led to the writing of this book. May God bless you as you find your joy in life. Thank you, and I love you!

TABLE OF CONTENTS

GLORIFYING GOD
LIFE LESSON #1

BIRTHDAY TRADITIONS ARE AS UNIQUE AS THE people who observe them. Several years ago, I began a personal tradition of giving a gift to someone on my birthday, especially the decade birthdays. I felt it was a way I could thank God for my birth.

The gift I planned for my 70th birthday was to post a short Life Lesson daily on my Facebook Timeline during the week that led up to my birthday. Each Life Lesson would represent a decade of my life.

I was not prepared for the thrilling response I received from Facebook Friends. They asked that I continue posting the Life Lessons so they could use them as devotionals. I knew my schedule would not allow me to write a new one daily, so after that first week, I expanded the Life Lessons into teaching devotionals and posted one weekly on Thursday mornings. A friend from my hometown coined the phrase, "Thursdays with Joy." Another friend hash-tagged Thursday mornings as "twj."

The readers requested the book you now hold in your hands. A Facebook Friend even suggested the title, "Finding Joy," and really that is the theme of the book. As a play on words with my name, *Joy*, it represents the Life Lessons I've learned while discovering who I am, but more importantly, Whose I am. God is at the center of each Life Lesson because, apart from Him, there is no true joy in life.

The Life Lessons span a period of time which included the annual holidays. However, the lessons are applicable whether or not they coincide with a specific holiday.

The following is the first Life Lesson posted on September 26, 2016:

I can hardly believe I will turn 70 this coming Sunday. (Remember: 70 is the new 50.) So, I decided each day this week I would post a Life Lesson I've learned during these years. I hope they will be meaningful to someone out there.

God created us and placed us on this beautiful earth to glorify Him (Isaiah 43:7). Of course, God is all-glorious. We can't make Him any more glorious than He already is, but we can reflect His glory to the people around us. In other words, we can show the world how wonderful He is. My prayer is through what I say or do--and what I refrain from saying or doing--I can glorify our marvelous Lord!

The Key to Inner Peace
Life Lesson #2

FORGIVENESS IS A KEY TO INNER PEACE. HOLDING on to hurts and/or resentments will block the flow of the Holy Spirit in our lives. Failure to forgive only hurts us. The people who have wronged us probably don't even think about what they've done.

But, when we continue to think about the offense--or perceived offense--we allow the offenders to hurt us again and again, and that gives them too much power in our lives.

Gandhi once said, "The weak can never forgive. Forgiveness is the attribute of the strong." So, let's be strong! Let's be forgivers! Besides, most of the time people don't intentionally do things *against* us, they do things *for* themselves.

Jesus knew this. That's why He could pray from the cross, *'Father, forgive them, for they do not know what they are doing'* (Luke 23:34).

The High Road
Life Lesson #3

ALWAYS CHOOSE TO TAKE THE HIGH ROAD. MANY reasons exist for doing so. For one, it's not as crowded because so many people travel on the low road.

Another reason to take the high road is it is not encumbered with regrets. Yes, it's more difficult to take the road less traveled, but the high road is always paved with peace.

Finally, the best reason to take the high road is it's closer to heaven, and what could be more wonderful?

Do I always travel the high road? Certainly not. However, I want to make it a personal goal to do so more often these next 70 years.

The best way to get on the high road is to give everyone the benefit of the doubt, and don't let people drag you down to a lower road. We never know what other people are going through in their lives that causes them to act the way they do.

Jesus realized we would deal with difficult people. In fact, He taught it is impossible to live without being offended (Luke 17:1). When we are offended by other people, the way we handle those offenses sets us on the journey of which road we will travel.

In the words of one of my favorite songs, "Your Love Keeps Lifting Me Higher." Let love lift us to the high road.

God's Decorations
Life Lesson #4

IN THE WEE HOURS OF THE MORNING SEVERAL YEARS ago, I woke up thinking about the Scripture verse John 3:16. I suddenly wondered what the Greek definition of the word "world" meant in that verse. I quietly got up so I wouldn't awaken Wayne or the girls, and I went into the study to look it up.

What I found brought tears to my eyes! "World" is *kosmos*, and it means "an orderly arrangement; adornment" [i.e. decoration]. Inherent in this word is the beautiful fact God created the world [an orderly arrangement], and He placed us in it [an adornment or decoration]. God did not consider His world complete without each of the decorations He hand-made and strategically placed in his or her proper place.

That realization brought me to my knees. I could hardly fathom the fact God did not consider His world complete without me. (The same is true of you!) Then I wondered if I really shine as brightly as the decoration He created me to be. I began to seek how I could become a better decoration.

The answer struck me one day. In life there are times when we all need help from others to be our best. Life's circumstances can tarnish us and cause us to become broken. I realized I shine most brightly in this world when I help others become the best decorations they can be.

In helping another person shine his or her decoration, my own takes on a brighter glow. So, I say to all of us as decorations fashioned by the hand of Almighty God, "Shine on!"

Where Is Your Heart?
Life Lesson #5

AFTER ADAM SINNED, HE HID FROM GOD'S PRES-
ence. When God came to commune with Adam *in the cool of the day*, He
asked, *'Adam, where are you'* (Genesis 3:8-9)?

God asked a rhetorical question because He knew where Adam was.
God is omnipotent (all-powerful), omnipresent (everywhere all the time),
and omniscient (all-knowing.) Some scholars say a better Hebrew rendering
of the question is, "Adam, where is your heart?"

God is asking each of us today the same question: "Where is your heart?"
What is filling our hearts that would replace God's rightful place there? Is it
another person? Is it a hidden sin? Is it jealousy, greed, lust, power, material
things, emotional wounds?

Blaise Paschal, the French mathematician/philosopher, spoke of how
empty our hearts are apart from God. Paschal said, "this infinite abyss can
be filled only with an infinite and immutable object; in other words, by
God himself."

Several years ago I learned something so beautiful it took my breath
away. In Hebrew, there is a letter--*shin*--that, when used alone, stands for
Almighty God (El Shaddai.) The outline of a cross-section of the human
heart reveals our hearts are in the shape of that letter! Let that marvelous
truth sink in for just a moment. Not only are we hand-made decorations
fashioned by Almighty God, but also our hearts are formed in the shape of
His own name. No one and no thing can adequately fill that shape, only God
Himself. Oh, blessed El Shaddai! Oh, glorious Almighty God!

So, I simply ask the same question God asked Adam many years ago,
"Where is your heart?"

The *Shin*

Echogram of the
Human Heart

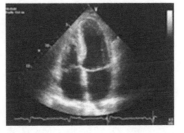

ARE YOU ALIVE?
LIFE LESSON #6

LIFE...WHAT AN AMAZING WORD! ONE SOURCE defines it as "the existence of a human being." However, I've personally noticed there is a big difference between *life* and *existence*.

Too many times I've rushed through my life merely existing. However, it doesn't take much to change existence back into life. I've found simple things can make the difference.

I mean, simple things like taking time to look (really look) at the world---and the people--around us; expressing gratitude; doing Random Acts of Kindness; basking in God's presence; walking barefoot through the grass; watching a sunrise or a sunset; listening to music; dancing; spending time with family and friends; reading a good book; laughing.

My husband, Wayne, says "if" is half of life (l-if-e). One day I noticed the *if* of life is encircled by *el,* a Hebrew name for God. (Hebrew reads from right to left.) God truly surrounds life with His presence.

So, I challenge us all to take time to experience life and not mere existence. We only get one chance at it, and each new day counts toward the totality of what our life will be. Jesus came so we could live life in the fullest sense of the word (John 10:10). So, I simply say, "Enjoy your life!"

Two Birthdays
Life Lesson #7

Mark Twain (one of my favorite authors) once said, "The two most important days in your life are the day you were born and the day you find out why." Well, 70 years ago today I was born. Eight years later I found out why.

Our church was in the midst of revival services. On that Wednesday night, I came home with a heavy heart. I realized during the service even though I was young, I was a sinner, and only Jesus could save my soul. I asked my father to help me understand what it all meant. The cherished scene that unfolded will remain in my heart forever. It was a cold night, so he sat with me by the space heater in our hall and explained how to have a relationship with God by accepting the forgiveness offered through Jesus's death on the cross. Then, he knelt with me beside that same heater, and I prayed the prayer that changed my life forever.

Even though I was young and did not understand deep theological truths, I understood enough to know my life could only have meaning through loving and serving God. Little did I know that night would open doors of opportunity to serve in far away places sharing the message with others.

I thank God I was born. I thank Him even more I was reborn through His Spirit. Please, if you've only been born once, don't put off the decision to be born again (John 3:7). The second birth is why you were born in the first place. With love!

WHISPERS IN THE STORM
LIFE LESSON #8

LESS THAN TWO WEEKS AGO, HURRICANE MATTHEW hit our area. Although it was labeled a Category One, it was one of the most vicious storms I've personally experienced. The effects of Matthew are heart-breaking. Even now, many people are displaced due to flooding, damage, and loss of property.

Sooner or later, we all go through storms in life. However, it may not be a hurricane. It may be a health crisis; a financial problem; a troubled relationship; the death of someone we love; the death of a dream; the loss of a job or career; feeling betrayed; losing faith in someone we trusted; losing faith in God.

One of my friends, Judy, says, "Storms clean and expose." Think about that statement a moment. It's simple, yet it's profound.

Just as physical storms stir things up and expose dead tree limbs, debris that needs to be removed, even weak places in homes or other structures, personal storms also expose areas that need our attention.

What are your personal storms exposing? Have you become more reliant on yourself (or someone else) than on God? Have you harbored un-forgiveness in your heart that will lead to bitterness, if it has not already done so? Have you drifted from your "first love," Jesus Christ? Have you made things more important in your life than the spiritual disciplines that bring you closer to God? Have you given up when God says, "endure to the end?"

Let the storms of your life do what storms do best: expose and clean! If you ask God to reveal debris in your heart, He will show you what needs to be cleaned out and cleared away. Then, allow the Holy Spirit to cleanse those areas. Believe me, I know from personal experience, nothing is more wonderful than a heart freshly cleansed by God!

On a regular basis, I have to allow the Holy Spirit to expose and clean my heart. Often, the debris has become such a part of my life, it's hard to let it go. I feel some of my debris is justified, and anyone would feel the way I do. Yet God whispers, "Let it go." When I do, the hush of God's sweet peace fills my heart.

The atmosphere after Hurricane Matthew was quiet, clear, and beautiful. Such beauty is available to us once we've dealt with the effects of our storms. As the Psalmist said, *He stilled the storm to a whisper; the waves of the sea were hushed* (Psalm 107:29). God is whispering through the storms of your life. Are you listening?

We Are Family
Life Lesson #9

IN THE LATE SEVENTIES, FOUR SISTERS, "SISTERS Sledge," recorded the popular song "We Are Family." It continues to be a hit song, and its catchy rhythm makes you want to get up and dance. You are probably singing it to yourself with your feet moving right now as you think about it.

Family is very strong on my mind right now. Last weekend my family gathered at Pretty Place near Table Rock, South Carolina as my great-niece, Kelli, married the love of her life in a beautiful wedding ceremony. The purity of their love for God and for each other was a testimony to us all. The wedding was followed by a festive reception where we as family, and friends who are like family, laughed, talked, reminisced, and happily watched the next generation having fun on the dance floor. It was a time of rejoicing.

The next day we traveled to Roanoke Rapids, North Carolina for the funeral of Wayne's cousin, Mary Vanice. His family gathered to honor her memory and to comfort each other as they shared her influence in each of their (our) lives. It was a time of sorrow.

In four day's time we experienced a new life beginning, and a well-lived life ending. Two constants were with us in each situation: *God* and *family*.

God places a very high premium on family. In fact, the family was God's first institution. He gave instructions in His Word concerning how families should function. However, too often selfishness enters the picture, and families become separated over differing opinions, jealousy, or material things.

I am so thankful for my family--my husband, our daughters and their husbands, and our precious grandchildren. I am also thankful for my sister, Lynn, and her family (who are also like my own.) And, I thank God for my extended family and friends who are chosen family.

I'd like to share a few observations I've learned about families in the 49 years of ministry Wayne and I have enjoyed together. Do you need to work on any of these?

1. **We as families should make time to stay connected**. Life can get so busy and schedules can become so hectic, family time

suffers. Planning family gatherings is key to ensuring we remain (or become) close.

2. **No family is perfect, so we must learn to forgive.** If you look at families in the Bible, you see that most, if not all, were dysfunctional in some way. Yet, God never gave up on families. Whatever your family relationships are at this point, determine not to dwell on the past. You can't undo anything, so do your part to ensure a brighter future.

3. **No matter what, your family is your family.** When the Bible says a man and wife shall be "joined" together, the word indicates they will be glued so tightly to each other, they cannot be separated without causing damage to each one. The same is true of our family unit as a whole. We are glued together by our blood line, or by commitments we have made to each other, and we should determine to do our part to keep the family unit in tact.

4. **Families are fun!** Families are made up of people with different personalities, different interests, different opinions, but those differences help keep things interesting. God often brings opposites together to create balance in relationships. Did you ever think God made all your family members different so you could maintain balance in your family?

So why not call or write a relative you haven't spoken to in a while? Ask God to show you if you need to reach out in reconciliation with any family members. Take time right now to thank God for your family (even if you're not the "Leave it to Beaver" family), and pray for specific needs family members might have.

Yes, "We Are Family," and so are you and your family!

On Being Real
Life Lesson #10

HALLOWEEN TOOK PLACE THIS PAST WEEK. I WAS amazed by some of the creative costumes I saw. For a few hours on a beautiful autumn night, people of all ages pretended to be someone (or something) they were not as they went from door to door repeating the now famous phrase, "Trick or Treat."

It has become an annual practice on this night to try to fool people by disguising who you really are. "Being real" is not the Halloween norm. In fact, "being real" is hardly the norm in daily life anymore.

At one time, people were as good as their word. What you saw was what you got. People could be trusted--or not trusted--on the basis of their actions.

How different the world is now! We are days away from an election where so much slander and so many lies have been spewed, we have a hard time discerning what is truth, and what is a campaign strategy. I long to know what is real, and what is truth, so I can make wise decisions with my voting.

I also long to know what is real, what is truth, with people whom I encounter on a regular basis. I must admit I am sometimes blindsided by people who have appeared to be one way, but in essence they were not real. Symbolically, it's as though they dressed in a Halloween costume and completely fooled me.

Every person reading this probably can relate to this Life Lesson in some way. I think I can safely say that most, if not all, of us have been hurt by someone who pretended to be one way, but in their hearts they were another way. If I could, I would wrap my arms around you as readers and protect you from hypocritical people. But I can't do that.

However, I can help you learn to recognize people who can cause you a great deal of hurt and emotional suffering. Several years ago, a close friend shared a very powerful article with me. I want to encourage you to look up the whole article and read all the scriptures and examples contained in the article. I will include a small summary here. Jesus said, *'Then you will know the truth, and the truth will set you free'* (John 8:32).

5 Indicators of an Evil Heart
By Leslie Vernick
www.biblestudytools.com/blogs/association-of-biblical-counselors/5-indicators-of-an-evil-and-wicked-heart.html

1. **Evil hearts are experts at causing confusion and contention.** (They twist facts, mislead, lie, avoid taking responsibility, make up stories, and withhold information.)
2. **Evil hearts are experts at fooling others with their smooth speech and flattering words.** (But if you look at the fruit of their lives, you will find no real evidence of godly growth or change.)
3. **Evil hearts crave and demand control, and their highest authority is their own self-reliance.** (They reject feedback and accountability and make up their own rules. They use scripture to their own advantage and avoid passages that might require self-correction and repentance.)
4. **Evil hearts play on the sympathies of good-willed people, often trumping the grace card.** (They demand warmth and forgiveness from others, but they have no empathy for those they've hurt, and they have no desire or intention to change.)
5. **Evil hearts have no conscience, no remorse.** (They don't struggle with sin, but they delight in it, all the while masquerading as someone of noble character.)

A warning: Only God can judge a heart. Judging someone else's heart is not our right or our responsibility. However, we can protect ourselves from hurt when we're aware of situations we need to avoid.

First, determine if any of the indicators describe your own heart, and bring your heart before God. Until the Spirit of God changes our hearts, we all have evil hearts. *The heart is deceitful above all things, and desperately sick; who can understand it* (Jeremiah 17:9 ESV)?

Secondly, listen carefully to the words of the one(s) you suspect may have an evil heart. Eventually his or her words will trip them up. *But the* *things that come out of a person's mouth come from the heart, and these defile them* (Matthew 15:18 ESV).

Thirdly, look carefully at the person's actions. Do they preserve their own position in life, or do they glorify God? *Above all else guard your heart, for everything you do flows from it* (Proverbs 4:23).

For those in your life who appear to have an evil heart, pray for them. You can't change them, so don't even try. However, you can pray and ask God to show them He loves them. They don't have to pretend to be what they are not. The truth of who they really are, coupled with God's love, can set them free!

Halloween is over. It's time to take off the disguises and masquerades and walk in truth. As we say here in the south, and I mean this as a prayer, "Bless your heart!"

Indivisible
Life Lesson #11

I pledge allegiance to the Flag of the United States of America, and to the Republic for which it stands, one Nation under God, indivisible, with liberty and justice for all.

HISTORY WAS MADE THIS WEEK IN THE ELECTION OF 2016. Donald J. Trump, a wealthy businessman, defeated Hillary Rodham Clinton, a long-time politician, in the presidential election. Today, some hearts are rejoicing, and other hearts are breaking.

This election has been brutal. I personally have never experienced such a divisive election in my lifetime.

I read the Pledge of Allegiance many times during this election week. One word repeatedly claimed my attention: *indivisible* (meaning "unable to be divided or separated.") Yet, on this day, our nation is sorely divided.

So, how do we move from where we are (divided) to where we need to be (united)? The answer can be found in the words that precede *indivisible...one Nation under God.*

I'm always amused as young children recite our Pledge of Allegiance when they get to the word "indivisible." Some interesting and amusing words come out instead. I remember in 1954 when the words "under God" were added. I had memorized the pledge and had my own mispronunciation of *indivisible*. When I'd get to the end of the pledge, I'd have to go back and repeat it so I could include the newly added words, *under God*. It took awhile for the addition to become a natural part of my recitation.

Even though the words were added as a response to the threat of communism, I'm so thankful they were added. I believe with all my heart the only way this great gulf in our nation can be healed is *under God*.

Years ago, King David wrote, *Blessed is the nation whose God is the Lord* (Psalm 33:12).

So, what does a nation *under God* look like?

A nation *under God* honors Him and keeps His commandments. It's just that simple. The result? *Liberty and justice for all.*

I close with a quote one of my favorite presidents included in his 2nd Inaugural address. The Civil War, a deadly war that severely divided the nation, would soon end. Yet, these words are as true today as when he first spoke them.

"The prayers of both could not be answered. That of neither has been answered fully. The Almighty has His own purposes. . . with malice toward none, with charity for all, with firmness in the right as God gives us to see the right, let us strive on to finish the work we are in, to bind up the nation's wounds." Abraham Lincoln

GIVE THANKS
LIFE LESSON #12

Give thanks in all circumstances, for this is God's will for you in Christ Jesus (I Thessalonians 5:18).

WE SPEND A LARGE PART OF OUR LIVES TRYING TO find God's will for our lives. Somehow the concept of God's will has taken on an illusive quality that leads us to believe His will is hard to discover or discern. Yet today's verse from I Thessalonians succinctly clarifies God's will: *Give thanks in all circumstances.*

Thankfulness is Christ-likeness. God uses it to help us find the right path on the journey of life. A thankful heart embraces the goodness all around and does not dwell on the negative side of people and/or circumstances. That quality in itself helps us walk in Jesus' footsteps, for His life was one of gratitude.

So, if we are to be thankful in all circumstances, how can we give thanks in circumstances that are not what we would like for them to be? A good start is to meditate and act on Psalm 100:5: *For the Lord is good; His mercy is everlasting, and His truth endures to all generations* (NJKV).

1. **We can be thankful because God is good. He cannot be any other way except good.** If our circumstances cause us to doubt God's fairness, focus on His goodness. List God's attributes that prove to you He is good. Remember, in the words of Charles Haddon Spurgeon, "God is too good to be unkind, and He is too wise to be mistaken. And when we cannot trace His hand, we must trust His heart."
2. **We can be thankful because God is merciful, and nothing can ever change that.** Because of His mercy, He paid the penalty for our sin and died in our place. As the Southern gospel song says, "He paid a debt He did not owe! I owe a debt I could not pay!" Such mercy, such love!
3. **We can be thankful because God's truth endures forever.** God's truth can help us see how He is working in all circumstances even when we are hurt or confused. His truth will set us free from bondages, including wrong perceptions of circumstances.

What is the best way we can show God we are thankful for His goodness, mercy, and truth regardless of our circumstances? The answer lies in Hebrews 13:1: *Through Jesus, therefore, let us continually offer to God a sacrifice of praise--the fruit of lips that openly profess His name.*

Roland Allen told the story of a medical missionary who worked in a region of the world where the people suffered from progressive blindness. They were born with healthy vision, but over time they lost their sight. The missionary miraculously developed a treatment that could stop the progression of the disease and save their eyesight.

The missionary said no one ever said, "thank you" for what he had done. Later he found out the phrase "thank you" was not in their vocabulary. Instead, they used a phrase that meant, "I will tell your name." Wherever they went, they shared the name of the missionary who had cured them.

So it is with us. One of the best ways we can say "Thank You" to God is to offer the sacrifice of the fruit of our lips, to *openly profess His name.*

Happy Thanksgiving! And, may God bless you!

SEARCH MY HEART
LIFE LESSON #13

Search me, O God, and know my heart...(Psalm 139:23).

HAVE YOU EVER LONGED FOR GOD? I MEAN *REALLY* longed for Him so desperately you didn't know what to do?

I became a believer as a child. My new-found faith was so precious to me, I wanted to share it with everyone. The sentences I'd write with my spelling words told the gospel. I was at church every time the doors were open. I would go with the adults on church visitation nights. I'd look around the sanctuary during the hymn of invitation at the end of the service, and if I saw someone who seemed to be wrestling with God, I'd leave my pew and ask if they wanted me to walk down the aisle with them. Looking back on those days, I admit I was probably exuberant to the point of being obnoxious to the people around me--especially the adults.

With time, I noticed my exuberance seemed the exception rather than the rule. So, I began to temper my enthusiasm trying to fit in to a more normal expression of faith. To paraphrase what the late Vance Havner said: "As Christians we are so subnormal that if we ever got back to the New Testament normal we would seem to people to be abnormal."

The above scripture from Psalm 139 became critical to my spiritual life when I was in my late twenties and early thirties. I found myself at a place in life where my original passion had waned, and I felt I was in a dry place in the desert spiritually speaking. I was so hungry for God I could hardly bear it.

Externally, I had every reason to be happy--a wonderful husband, two precious daughters, a loving extended family, great friends, and various interests. Yet, nothing filled the hunger I felt, and I longed to regain my original spiritual passion.

I sought God day and night. I could truly relate to the words of Psalm 42:1: *As the deer pants after streams of water so my heart pants for you, my God.*

God used several factors converging to help me find the peace I so desperately sought. I found myself in a group of fellow seekers. We were a motley crew indeed—from the head of the Religion Department of a major university, to a man fresh from living on the streets, to anything and everything in between. We all came together weekly for one purpose—we desired a deeper walk with God.

In my quest, God led me to Catherine Marshall's book, <u>Something More</u>. Her chapter on forgiveness was the missing piece of the puzzle to me. For the first time, I realized the reason I felt so far from God was the un-forgiveness in my heart (which I was not even aware was there.) The un-forgiveness blocked the flow of the Holy Spirit in my life. Yes, I was a Christian. Yes, I had all of God (Father, Son, and Holy Spirit) in my life, but the things I unknowingly harbored in my heart quenched the Holy Spirit like a clogged pipe under a sink.

Shortly thereafter, I sat down with a legal pad and pencil. I asked God to search my heart and show me anything that blocked my fellowship with Him. As He exposed it to me, I wrote it down.

I could not believe all the things He revealed. I was shocked to think all of that *stuff* had been living inside of me. Most of the things on the list were easy to forgive because of time and distance from the offense, and so I did. However, with a few of them, I felt justified in feeling the way I did. Yet, I knew, *you must forgive*.

Finally, I got a red pen for the blood of Jesus, and as I took those offenses symbolically out of my heart and lifted them up to God using sign language, I wrote, "I forgive you" across each one.

It is hard to describe the peace that flooded my soul. The Bible took on a new relevance for me. I stood in church singing hymns with tears streaming down my face because the words now were so meaningful. I had more power in witnessing.

However, I had not *arrived*, I had only *begun*. The need to search our hearts is not a one-time thing. It's a practice we need to repeat as often as necessary. It truly is life-changing!

Next lesson...some practical steps toward extending and receiving forgiveness.

EXTENDING AND RECEIVING FORGIVENESS
LIFE LESSON #14

'. . . then neither do I condemn you,' Jesus declared. 'Go now and leave your life of sin' (John 8:11).

WHEN WAYNE PREACHES ON THIS SCRIPTURE FROM the story of the adulterous woman, he points out the woman in the scripture had to experience three aspects of forgiveness in order to be free:

1. Accepting God's forgiveness,
2. Extending forgiveness to her accusers,
3. Forgiving herself.

Which of the three aspects of forgiveness do you find most difficult in your life? If you are like I am, it probably changes with different circumstances.

This morning, Wayne asked me why I'm writing so much on forgiveness. "Do you need to forgive someone?"

I laughed and said, "No one I'm aware of." I then explained these are lessons I've learned, or am learning, throughout the whole of life. This lesson is an on-going one in my life and, I believe, in the lives of most people.

Sometimes it's easy to forgive. Other times it's more difficult. The need to forgive seems directly correlated to the depth of pain caused by the offense or the perceived offense.

- **If we are the offender, we need to pray for the strength to confess our wrong to the person(s) involved and seek his or her forgiveness.** I recently, heard Evangelist Frank Shivers make a statement that resonated with me.
  "As wide as the sin, as wide should be the confession."

- **If we are the offended, we need the Holy Spirit's help in discerning whether or not we can truly forgive the person through prayer, or if we need to talk with them about what happened.**

- **If we are having a hard time forgiving ourselves, we need to search our hearts to find out why.** Satan often uses this aspect of forgiveness to keep us in bondage to the things God--and others--have long since forgiven us: *It is for freedom that Christ has set us free. Stand firm, then, and do not let yourselves be burdened again by a yoke of slavery* (Galatians 5:1).

I am not trying to over-simplify a very important concept, or relegate it to a formula, but I learned a pattern from <u>Victorious Christian Living</u> that is very helpful to me when it comes to forgiveness. I hope it will help you as well.

1. **State the offense or the perceived offense.**
2. **How did it make you feel?** (Get real during this section. Did it make you feel rejected, betrayed, unimportant, etc.?)
3. **What were the ramifications of the offense?** (Did you lose a job, a friendship, sustain a financial loss, etc.?)
4. **Did it cause you to sin?** (Did you gossip, demean the person, seek revenge, etc.?)

Christmas is all about forgiving. The manger of Bethlehem led to the cross of Calvary. In scripture, forgiveness is never presented as an option, it is always a command. God bless you in your journey of extending and receiving forgiveness.

In the next lesson, "Back to the Future," we will look at how God uses the experiences of the past and present to prepare us for our futures. The perfect example is found in the manger of Bethlehem!

Back to the Future
Life Lesson #15

And she brought forth her firstborn son, and wrapped him in swaddling clothes, and laid him in a manger; because there was no room for them in the inn (Luke 2: 7 KJV).

And the angel said unto them, 'Fear not: for behold I bring you good tidings of great joy, which shall be to all people' (Luke 2:10 KJV).

GOD TAKES THE EXPERIENCES OF THE PAST TO prepare us for our futures. I first realized this as a young minister's wife.

I was born in Baltimore, Maryland and grew up in a row house until shortly before my sixth birthday when we moved to South Carolina. Then, when I was thirteen, my parents helped start a church in my hometown, Gaffney. (It's now the beautiful Central Baptist Church.) The new church met in our home for almost two years.

Those experiences helped prepare me for the day God called Wayne and me to leave a growing, thriving church in the south and re-locate to serve as pastor of a mission-type church in New Jersey. We did not have a typical church building, so we met in a Grange Hall for services. Only then did I realize God had used the experiences of my upbringing to prepare me for this new calling.

The same is true of the events in Bethlehem on that special holy night when the Christ-child was born. All the events of His birth were later present at His death and resurrection. What an amazing God we serve Who declared *the end from the beginning* (Isaiah 46:10 KJV)!

One day while deep in thought about Luke 2:7, it occurred to me everything in this verse about Jesus' birth was a foreshadowing of His death, burial, and resurrection.

And she	The "she" in this verse was prophesied as early as Genesis 3:15. Every person in the Bible is referred to as the "seed of man," but the Child of the woman in this passage is referred to as "the seed of woman" since her Child was conceived by the Holy Spirit and not an earthly father.
Firstborn Son	The perfect sacrifice or gift was a male animal of the first year (Exodus 12:5).
Wrapped Him in swaddling clothes.	At His burial Jesus was wrapped in clean linen clothes (John 19:40).
Laid in a manger	He was laid in a hewn tomb (Matthew 27:60).
He was born in a borrowed stable because there was no room in the inn.	Jesus was buried in a borrowed tomb (Matthew 27:60).
An angel announced Jesus' birth	An angel announced His resurrection (Matthew 28:5-6).

Remember: God sees the end from the beginning. Even in ways you may not understand, He is setting events in place to prepare you for your future: *And we know that all things work together for good to them that love God, to them who are the called according to His purpose* (Romans 8:28 KJV).

God bless you as you look back over your own life and see how this principle is true.

From the Manger to the Cross
Life Lesson #16

But Mary treasured up all these things and pondered them in her heart (Luke 2:19).

Previously, we looked at how God uses the experiences of the past (and present) to prepare us for the future. Today's Life Lesson is a very emotional one for me. In fact, as I sat down to write it, tears filled my eyes. I cannot imagine what Mary felt as she held her newborn baby in her arms.

All the things that happened—giving birth to her firstborn child in a stable in Bethlehem, angels announcing his birth, shepherds coming to pay homage, all the events of her baby's birth—were not only extraordinary, but also they were foretold by the prophets.

Growing up in a Jewish home, Mary would have known the scriptures about the Messiah. One of the main prophesies was the Messiah would be born through a virgin (Genesis 3:15, Isaiah 7:14). Mary knew she had *known no man* (Luke 1:34), and the child she carried inside her for nine months was conceived by the Holy Spirit. She held Him in her arms, and the indescribable love between a mother and child filled her heart.

She also knew the Messiah's birthplace would be Bethlehem. Mary lived in Nazareth. The fact her baby was born in Bethlehem was one more indication she had given birth to the promised Messiah. Many more scriptures and prophesies also were fulfilled at His birth.

Mary pondered these things in her heart. "Pondered" actually means "to bring together in one's mind; to confer with one's self." As she felt the joy of holding her tiny child close to her heart, she remembered the prophesies that foretold how He would suffer and die to atone for the sins of the world. She pondered, putting pieces of the puzzle together.

For, you see, the manger led to the cross. He, who was now Mary's son, would one day become her Savior. Although she did not know when or how it would happen, she *treasured up all these things and pondered them in her heart.*

Several years ago, as I *pondered* what Mary must have experienced as a mother, I felt deep sorrow. As a result, I wrote the following poem. I pray it will bless you as you consider anew that the Child in the manger became the Savior on the cross.

The Shadow of the Cross

The shadow of the cross was upon the manger there,
As Mary held her baby close and wonder filled the air.
A night of joy, a night of peace, now gone were all her fears.
But did she know, as she held Him close, her joy would turn to tears?

Shepherds gazing, angels singing, gold, frankincense and myrrh,
All of these must have been very strange to her.
How could she know as she pondered them and kept them in her heart,
That each one would, at the end of His life, come to play a part?

Shepherds watching over sheep--He would be God's own Lamb.
Costly gifts of burial spices accompanied Him to His tomb.
Angels singing, "He's not here! He's risen from the dead!"
Could she have known that all of these were as the prophets said?

Gentle Mary, meek and mild--chosen for joy and for sorrow.
Enjoy tonight, hold memories tight, don't worry about tomorrow.
Just hold your baby close to you, tonight you gave birth to the Christ.
But, the shadow of the cross is there--and will be all His life.

What I've Learned from the Wise Men
Life Lesson #17

FOR YEARS I FELT I HAD MISSED SOMETHING IN THE story of the "Wise Men" or magi (Matthew 2:1-12). Through research and various sermons and teachings, I learned they may not have come to the stable after Jesus's birth, but they probably got to Bethlehem at a later time.

Also, we have no idea how many magi actually came. The number three probably was introduced because of the three recorded gifts they gave.

Most of the emphasis through the years centered on the gifts the magi brought. Many commentators see symbolism in the three gifts presented to the Christ child--gold for His royalty, frankincense representing His role as the High Priest (burning incense was a part of the priestly duty), and the burial spice, myrrh, representing His impending death and burial.

This year I prayerfully read and re-read Matthew 2:1-12. I asked God what I had missed, and what message in the visit of the Wise Men could help me in the coming new year.

About the third time through, the scripture became illuminated in my heart. For the first time, I saw a pattern I hope to be faithful in following this new year. It's simple, yet profound.

- **The Wise Men joyfully sought Jesus:** *And when they saw the star they were overjoyed* (Matthew 2:10).

This year, more than ever, I want to joyfully seek Jesus. I want to look for ways He is working in my life and in the lives of those around me--and rejoice when I see Him at work. I want to study the scriptures and find more amazing things about Him--and rejoice when I find them. I want to seek His presence more consistently than ever--and rejoice when I'm aware of Him.

I will always find Jesus if I seek Him. He is on every page of the Bible. He is in every breath I take. He is everywhere all the time. However, I often become focused on life itself, and I fail to seek the Source of my life. He longs for me to seek Him. In fact, He promises: *You will seek me and find me when you seek me with all your heart* (Jeremiah 29:13).

- **They worshiped Him.**

The Wise Men...*bowed down and worshiped Him* (Matthew 2:11). Then they presented their gifts to Jesus.

Exactly what is worship? The dictionary meaning is "adoring reverence or regard." However, the Greek word for worship captures the true beauty. *Proskunio* - "I go down on my knees." It is comprised of two words: *Pros* - "toward" + *kyneo* "to kiss." True worship is when in my heart, I bow down and kiss toward God letting Him know how much I love Him.

When our daughter, Molly, was in middle school, she excitedly told me about something that had happened. As she finished, she said, "Thank you, Jesus," and she blew a kiss toward heaven. Then, seeming somewhat embarrassed, she said, "Mama, sometimes I blow kisses to God. Do you think He minds?"

Fighting back tears, I said, "Honey, I'm sure He loves it very much."

Years later, when I looked up the Greek meaning for worship, I told Molly that her kisses toward God were actually high praise to Him.

This year, as I joyfully seek and find Him, I want to offer Him the highest praise I know how to give. It may be as simple as bowing down and blowing Him kisses.

Because after all, "Wise Men (and women) still seek Him!" I want to be one of those!

What I've learned from the Wise Men (Part 2)
The Gift of Choosing Joy
Life Lesson #18

Continuing "What I've Learned from the Wise Men," I'd like to make one more point, so I decided to write a Part 2. You might want to re-read Life Lesson #17 and the story of the visit of the Wise Men to the Christ child as found in Matthew 2:1-12.

In the last lesson we saw that the Wise Men:

1. Joyfully sought Jesus
2. When they found Him, they worshipped Him.

The point for today is the magi also presented gifts to Him—gold, frankincense, and myrrh. I thought a lot this week about their gifts. All come from the earth. He created the world, so, whether they realized it or not, the magi offered back to Him gifts He already had given them. Jesus is the Great Recycler!

The same is true of our gifts today. Many things come to my mind as gifts we could offer Him: our lives, our hearts; our time, talents, and tithes; our love, faith, obedience...so many choices. But actually, He has already given us any gift we could ever offer back to Him. Isn't He wonderful?

However, the gift I want to focus on today is the gift of *choosing joy*, and it is a lesson I remind myself of often. Scriptures teach that joy is given to us once we come into a relationship with God. However, it will lie dormant inside us unless we choose to exercise it (Galatians 5:22). A thought came to me today: Just as obedience exercises our love, joy exercises our faith. When we choose joy, we let God know that we believe His word and have faith in Him: *And we know that in all things God works for the good of those who love him...*(Romans 8:28).

I enjoy my name, especially at Christmas time. (Actually, my name is Joyce, but I've been called Joy since I was born.) It is a constant reminder to look for things that cause joy in my heart. A few years ago I met an older man, and when I was introduced to him, he simply said, "Joy is the most infallible sign of the presence of God." His statement profoundly impacted my life. If you desire to be God's reflection in this world, choosing joy is a definite way. Joy is contagious!

However, we cannot fake joy. We might pretend to be happy, but true abiding, bubbling-forth joy can only come from a heart that has faith in God.

So, how do we get this joy? First, and foremost, we attain joy through a relationship with Jesus. He is the Joy-Giver.

Jesus first

Others second

Yourself last.

I've read and heard that this formula is the secret to joy. I do know the "Jesus first" part is true. Apart from Him, there is no joy.

Staying focused on Jesus keeps us from putting too much attention on the circumstances in our lives that might not be joyful. Researchers say 80% of what we encounter on any given day is negative, and 90% of what we tell ourselves is negative. If these statistics are true, we may have to look hard to see the positive, joyful things in our lives.

We each know in our hearts what we need to do to stay focused on Jesus. We also know the things in our lives (misplaced priorities, lack of interest, "busyness," laziness, etc.) that keep us from focusing on Him. It's a mixed-up world, and life sometimes gets hard, but the great Joy-Giver provides us with what we need to get through--not as victims, but as victors!

Last Thursday, we helped with the memorial service for one of the most joyful people I've ever met. Kathleen loved to laugh. Rarely, in all the years I've known her, did I see her without a smile. It was obvious she had learned the way to stay focused on Jesus, even in the midst of trials.

Kathleen had two sons who died around the age of 5 from a congenital disease. She later lost her beloved husband, Bill, followed by the death of their oldest son while he was still a young man. Even in the midst of all these circumstances, Kathleen found ways to remain joyful.

She was a prayer warrior. In fact, when she was in the hospital before her death, she wanted the doctors to dismiss her so she could go home and get back to her prayer station interceding for others.

Kathleen's daughter, Kathy, often says her mother chose joy. When she questioned Kathleen about how to remain joyful in difficult circumstances, Kathleen said, "You have to pray. Stay focused on Jesus. Develop 'calloused knees' through prayer." And Kathy is the perfect image of her mother in that way and in many other ways.

I'm thankful for such a beautiful example of joy. After all, *the joy of the Lord is your strength...* (Nehemiah 8:10). Don't we all want to be strong?

Let It Go
Life Lesson #19

The Disney movie *Frozen* is full of valuable lessons. I enjoyed watching it with our grandchildren. The theme song, "Let It Go," was not only powerful, but also it spoke directly to the issue of how to move forward in life.

The following scripture gives us clear instructions on how to *let it go*: *Forgetting what is behind and straining toward what is ahead, I press on toward the goal to win the prize for which God has called me heavenward in Christ Jesus* (Philippians 3:13b-14).

Forgetting what is behind. Paul hit the nail on the head with that phrase. The only way we can move on triumphantly is to let go of the past, except what we can learn from it.

Too many times we are bound so tightly to the past, or burdened so heavily with worries of the future, we miss the joy of the present. I enjoy the "Family Circle" cartoons. I saw one in which the older sister told her little brother, "Yesterday is the past; tomorrow is the future; today is a gift. That's why they call it 'the present.'" Wow! Each breath we take in the present is a gift.

As I thought about the above verse from Philippians (after studying To Live Is Christ by Beth Moore), I realized what Paul needed to forget, what he needed to let go of. I saw a pattern that speaks to us today.

So often we think of the Apostle Paul as being such a powerhouse, we forget he was also very human. I can almost hear the hurt in his heart as he talks about how we must *let it go*.

Look at some of the things Paul had to let go of, and see if any apply to your life.

- **Paul had to let go of his old mindset.**

He had been raised in extreme legalism. He was a *Hebrew of Hebrews; in regard to the law a Pharisee...* (Philippians 3:5) which meant he was 100% devoted to being a Pharisee. The Pharisees not only focused on the laws of God, but also they adhered to hundreds of man-made laws they believed defined God's laws. Those man-made laws were not only burdensome, but also they were impossible to obey.

However, as our amazing God ordained it, Paul became a student of Gamaliel. See Acts 5:27-39 to get a glimpse of Gamaliel's wisdom and grace. After Paul experienced God's grace on the road to Damascus, he understood his rabbi's example more fully, and his own life and teachings became all about grace.

- **Paul had to let go of the ways he had hurt others.**

He was responsible for the imprisonment and death of many of Jesus' followers (Acts 26:9-11). Horrible memories filled his mind, but he had to let them go in order to be all God intended him to be.

- **Paul had to let go of the ways he had been hurt by others.**

In each town Paul entered, he first preached Jesus in the synagogues. He often was ridiculed and abused for his teaching. He then moved on to preach the same message to the Gentiles. Five times Paul was given 39 stripes, 3 times beaten with rods, and even once stoned and left for dead. He had much to forgive and to let go of in order to persevere in what God called him to do.

- **Paul had to let go of his feelings of failure.**

You might be thinking that "Paul" and "failure" are two words that do not belong together. Yet we find in scripture at times he dealt with feelings of insecurity and failure.

Scholars agree Paul's sermon on Mars Hill in Athens, Greece, was one of the greatest examples of a message ever presented (Acts 17:22-32). His sermon was a perfect model for speaking to an audience. He spoke on things they could relate to by observing their surroundings. He gave a clear message of apologetics (defense of the faith.) Yet, as outstanding as Paul's message was, and as carefully chosen as his words were, he did not receive the reception he desired.

Some people mocked him; a small number became believers; a few indicated they wanted to hear more.

After he left Athens, he went to Corinth where, by his own admission, he did not come with *eloquence or human wisdom* (although both were evident in his sermon at Mars Hill), but rather with *weakness, great fear, and trembling* (I Corinthians 2:1; 3). At Corinth we see a broken and disappointed man relying only on *Jesus Christ and him crucified* (I Corinthians 2:2).

Do you need to let go of any of the things Paul had to release?

> Have you held on to flawed thinking or an erroneous worldview?
> Have you hurt someone?
> Have you been hurt by someone?
> Have you felt like a failure or a disappointment?

If so, it's time to *let it go*. You cannot clutch onto the past and reach for the future. You can only move in one direction. Which will it be?

Paul gives us the answer to how to let go. We must...*press on toward the goal to win the prize for which God has called me heavenward in Christ Jesus* (Philippians 3:13b-14).

Pressing toward heaven blurs the hurts of the past. So I ask, are you ready to *let it go*?

※

Just Say No
Life Lesson #20

This life lesson probably seems a bit contro-versial coming from a minister's wife. However, it is one of the most important lessons I've learned, and one I keep re-learning. I know this Life Lesson is meant for someone out there who will read it, and I hope it helps.

Come to me, all you who are weary and burdened, and I will give you rest. Take my yoke upon you and learn from me, for I am gentle and humble in heart, and you will find rest for your souls. For my yoke is easy and my burden is light (Matthew 11:28-30).

For many years I unknowingly equated busyness with godliness. I said "yes" to almost everything I was asked to do in the church and community. Interestingly, the more I said *yes*, the more people bragged on me for being busy. Naturally, I surmised I did the right thing by staying so busy.

One day I had a revelation that changed my life. I was tired from all I was doing. Plus, I found I had said *yes* to many things I didn't want to do. I felt compelled to do them because I didn't want to reject the person asking me. These things had become burdensome. On the other hand, the things I said *yes* to I felt God leading me to do were a complete joy. I realized if I *just say no* to the things I did not feel God leading me to do, I would have more time for Wayne and our daughters, more time to keep our home in order, more time to rest and refresh, and I would experience more joy in doing the things I did do.

I also realized if I said *yes* just to keep from hurting the feelings of the person asking me to do something, I might block the right person from getting that opportunity.

Jesus wants us to be busy about the Father's work as He was, but we find in scripture He knew how to *just say no* when necessary. Since He is our role model, let's look at a few instances where we can learn from the Master Teacher.

- **Jesus *just said no* even to good things.**
  Mark 1:34-38 shows Jesus refused to go back to Capernaum to continue healing and casting out demons. He told His disciples He must go to the next town and preach the Kingdom of God. Undoubtedly, He followed what He felt led to do, because He spent time alone with the Father.

- **Jesus *just said no* to trying to fix everyone's problems.**
  In Luke 12:13-15, He refused to become a part of an inheritance dispute. I love to help people, but I'm sure I probably get in God's way when I try to fix problems that are none of my business.

- **Jesus *just said no* to people who were trying to use Him.**
  In John 6:26-27, He sent a group of hungry people away telling them they wanted food from Him, but they needed spiritual renewal.

- **Jesus *just said no* to things that would make Him look good in the eyes of man.** In Luke 23:8-9, He refused to do the miracles Herod demanded because He knew Herod's motives were not pure.

These examples are just a few of the many times Jesus set boundaries in His life. So, how can we know when to *just say no*?

Once again, Jesus is our example. He often retreated alone to rest and to spend time communing with the Father. He did not do this because He was so exhausted He had to take a break, but He planned for these times. Thus, He knew what to accept or reject when it came to choices.

Also, if you look at Jesus' life, you see He was rarely in a hurry. Even though He had many busy days, He took life at a healthy pace. His busyness was balanced.

Just saying no when necessary; living at a healthy pace; most importantly, scheduling times alone with the Father: Is there an area of your life where you need to learn from the greatest role model of all times?

May God bless you and give you the courage to *just say no*!

KALEIDOSCOPE DAYS
LIFE LESSON #21

AREN'T KALEIDOSCOPES AMAZING? FOR AS LONG AS I can remember, I've been fascinated by how turning the end of the cylinder causes patterns and designs to immediately change.

I'm working on my first novel. (I'm trying to get serious about finishing it since the story lines for the sequel have formed in my mind.) It's a sweet inspirational love story.

In one of the early scenes, as the leading man and leading woman are getting to know each other, they discuss their perspectives on life. Sarah asks Bob to fill in the blanks after saying, "Life is..." He sits reflectively for a moment then replies, "Life is a series of well-thought-out decisions." Sarah laughs and says, "That's good--heavy--but good." When he asks her to do the same, she immediately replies, "Life is...like a kaleidoscope."

As he laughs, she explains her fascination with kaleidoscopes. She tells him how a person can sit and look at design after design. Some are pretty. Many are ordinary. Then you make one little turn of the cylinder, and a pattern appears that's so beautiful it takes your breath away. She goes on to say life is like the designs. Many moments and days are ordinary. Some are good. Some are even bad. But then, suddenly, a magnificent moment occurs that takes your breath away.

Ever since I wrote that part of the chapter, I've thought about ordinary versus extraordinary days. I may seem like a Pollyanna, but I want to find a way to make each day I'm on this earth an extraordinary day. God placed me in His beautiful world, He surrounded me with people I love and things I enjoy, and I feel it's my fault if I fail to recognize the magnificent among the mundane.

So, in my quest for the extraordinary, I found a wonderful nugget tucked away in 2 Kings 6:17, *And Elisha prayed, 'Open his eyes, LORD, so that he may see.' Then the LORD opened the servant's eyes, and he looked and saw the hills full of horses and chariots of fire all around Elisha.*

In this passage (2 Kings 6:11-17), the King of Assyria sent an army to capture Elisha and take him back as a prisoner. (The King believed Elisha was a spy, but God had revealed inside truths to the prophet about the

Assyrian army.) Enemies with chariots and weaponry filled the hills around Dothan during the night.

The next morning when Elisha's servant went outside, he saw the army and ran back to Elisha in panic mode. Elisha assured his servant with the words, *'Don't be afraid,' the prophet answered. 'Those who are with us are more than those who are with them'* (2 Kings 6:16).

Then Elisha prayed the short, but powerful prayer, found in 2 Kings 6:17 *'Open his eyes, LORD, so that he may see.'*

At that moment, God gave the servant a glimpse into the spiritual realm, and he saw an army of angels, horses, and chariots of fire, between them and the enemy army. Talk about extraordinary!

Through the years, I have found when I personalize Elisha's prayer and ask God to *'open my eyes so that I may see,'* I am much more aware of the extraordinary. I recognize more clearly God working in my life and in the lives of those around me. And, anytime I recognize God working, it is indeed extraordinary.

So, if you don't have a kaleidoscope, I encourage you to get one and enjoy looking for the designs so extraordinary they take your breath away.

I also encourage you to pray the short, powerful prayer that will help you recognize the extraordinary all around you in your life: *'Open my eyes, LORD, so that I may see.'*

One of my favorite quotes (although I cannot verify the source) is: "Life is not measured by the number of breaths we take, but by the moments that take our breath away."

Will you join me in the quest for Kaleidoscope Days--days in which we go through life looking for the extraordinary?

THIS TOO SHALL PASS
LIFE LESSON #22

I ONCE HEARD A STORY OF AN ELDERLY MAN WHO, IN spite of many trials in his life, had remained optimistic and strong. A younger man asked him the secret of his optimistic aging. The older man answered, "No matter what I'm going through in life--either good or bad--I just remind myself, 'This too shall pass.'"

He was right. Life has an ebb and flow that makes it what it is--life. If you are going through a bad time, *this too shall pass*. If you are going through a good time, *this too shall pass*.

Have you ever heard of The Adversity Principle? Simply stated, nothing can grow effectively in a perfect environment. From people to plants, we all need some challenges to help us grow and make us stronger. So if you are in a time of adversity, just remember, *this too shall pass*, and you will grow from the experience(s).

Although the phrase, "This too shall pass," is not in the Bible, scripture does validate the principle of the quote. The following scriptures encourage me during times I need to remind myself of this truth.

- *...weeping may endure for a night, but joy comes in the morning* (Psalm 30:5b NKJV).
- *For our light and momentary troubles are achieving for us an eternal glory that far outweighs them all. So we fix our eyes not on what is seen, but on what is unseen, since what is seen is temporary, but what is unseen is eternal* (2 Corinthians 4:17,18).
- *Because of the LORD's great love, we are not consumed, for his compassions never fail. They are new every morning; great is your faithfulness* (Lamentations 3:22-23).

The exact origin of the phrase, "This too shall pass," is not known. Some believe it was first mentioned in Persian Sufi Poetry. Others attribute it to a fable by King Solomon, although it is not included in the Bible. The fable goes as follows:

King Solomon wanted to teach one of his leaders, Benaiah, a lesson in humility. Even though Solomon knew there was no such thing as a magic ring in existence, the King sent Benaiah in search of such a ring. If a sad man looked at the ring, he would become happy. If a happy man looked at the ring, he would become sad. Solomon gave Benaiah six months to find the ring and present it to the King during the Feast of Sukkot.

Benaiah searched for months to no avail. The night before the great festival, he walked through a poor section of Jerusalem. He stopped to ask an elderly jeweler if he knew about such a ring. The jeweler quickly picked up a gold ring and engraved the words, "This too shall pass," in Hebrew on the ring.

The next day, Solomon asked Benaiah to come forward with the magic ring. He thought Benaiah would have to admit failure because he was unable to do what the king asked. Instead, Benaiah handed Solomon the ring.

When the king read the inscription, he was stunned and saddened. He realized all his wealth and possessions, his power, and even his life were temporary.

This too shall pass, is a powerful motivation to help us stay focused on what is temporal versus what is eternal--love!

BEAUTY IS IN THE EYE OF THE BEHOLDER
LIFE LESSON #23

WHEN WE LIVED IN BOONE, NORTH CAROLINA, MY special place to worship God was the Yadkin Valley Overlook on the Blue Ridge Parkway. I would drive there, put worship music in the CD player, open my car windows so I could hear the music, and sit on a rock and worship God. I'd sing, I'd pray, and I'd soak in the beauty of the mountains and valleys. I cannot tell you how special that place became to me.

A good friend came to visit us for a few days. One day during his visit, Wayne had some meetings at the church, so I took Ken to see some of the beautiful sights in the area. We went to Valle Crucis, Blowing Rock, and even enjoyed some "touristy" things.

Then I told him we were going to the most special place of all. I drove to my worship site, and we got out of the car. "Isn't this the most beautiful place you've ever seen?" I asked.

He slowly and reflectively said, "I'm sure it *could* be."

Then I realized what he meant. You see, it was winter. Hardly a leaf was on a tree. The landscape was barren and brown. *But*, I knew what it looked like in spring when the trees turned from the light green of new growth to the deep green hues of summer. I had seen it in the glorious splendor of fall with colors too beautiful to describe. Even in winter, I had seen the beauty of fresh snow on the trees.

So when I looked at the view, I associated it with beauty. When he looked, he saw only bareness. I started laughing, and I could hardly stop. I told him I knew he probably wondered when I talked about how beautiful it was. Then I described how it looked in the different seasons.

That day taught me a valuable lesson. I've always heard, "Beauty is in the eye of the beholder," and it really is. I based my opinion on the beauty of the overlook I had seen during the changing seasons. Ken based his impression on what he could see at that moment. My perception was that of beauty. His perception was that of stark bareness.

We tend to think when God looks at us He sees our flaws--our sins, our wrong choices, our disappointing behavior. The truth is, when God sees us, He sees us as beautiful. He doesn't see what we are as much as what He knows we can become. He sees us in light of who He created us to be.

Some of the scriptures that remind us of this fact are the following:

God saw all that He had made, and behold, it was very good...(Genesis 1:31).

God has made everything beautiful in its time...(Ecclesiastes 3:11).

...The LORD does not look at the things people look at. People look at the outward appearance, but the LORD looks at the heart...(I Samuel 16:7).

And even though this verse is about a couple in love, I believe it is symbolic of God's great love for us: *You are altogether beautiful, my darling; there is no flaw in you* (Song of Solomon 4:7).

I love the words of the song, "Something Beautiful." I think it speaks directly to this Life Lesson.

> *Something beautiful, something good;*
> *All my confusion, He understood.*
> *All I had to offer Him was brokenness and strife,*
> *But He made something beautiful of my life.*

Offer Him your life, regardless of what you think it looks like right now. He will make it beautiful as only He can do. Rest assured God can take the broken pieces of our lives and turn them into something beautiful. He takes us from bareness to beautiful!

Yes, *beauty is in the eye of the beholder.* Please never forget your Beholder loved you enough to die for you! Love like that is true beauty!

He Took My Place
Life Lesson #24

But God demonstrates his own love for us in this: while we were still sinners, Christ died for us (Romans 5:8).

I SPENT ONE OF THE BEST SUMMERS OF MY LIFE AS A teenager on summer staff at Ridgecrest Baptist Assembly (now called LifeWay Conference Center) near Black Mountain, North Carolina. Those of you who know me well know how I love that area of the Blue Ridge Mountains. My deep love for the mountains began that summer.

Then, for many years after we married, Wayne and I taught at Ridgecrest during youth week. We each had a class of about one hundred teenagers while our daughters, Meri Beth and Molly, were in the children's classes and activities. In addition, we took with us the youth group from whatever church we served at the time, so it was always a fun-filled week.

One year I had a boy, John, in my class along with his best friend, Ray. They were adorable teenagers, but John was the class cut-up, and I had to reel him in at times. He called me "Ma," and soon the whole group called me "Ma" no matter where they saw me on campus.

Throughout the week I asked God to show me the best way to express to the youth what Jesus' death on the cross meant to them personally. He gave me an idea that gives me chills each time I think of it. I asked John and Ray to stay after class for a few minutes. I explained the idea to them and asked if they would be willing to participate. They readily agreed.

The next day, we reached the culmination of the discussion on the atonement and Jesus' substitutionary death. Just before I drove home the main point, I gave the key phrase that was John's cue. He stood up and said, "Ma, this is boring," and he fell in the floor.

The youth gasped and sat horrified over what John had done. I then pretended to get angry at him, telling him he had disrupted the class all week, but his current action was more than I could stand. I ordered him back to his cottage to tell his chaperones he was sent out of class.

He tried to talk me out of it, but I sternly told him to go. You could have heard a pin drop on the carpeted floor. "Go!" I demanded.

Just as John got to the door, Ray stood up and said, "Ma, please. Let me go instead."

I explained that he could not go. John had done wrong, and John had to face the consequences.

Ray continued, "You don't understand, Ma. John has been in trouble with our chaperones all week, and if he goes back to our cottage, they'll send him home. He's my best friend, and I want to take his punishment for him."

John stood with his head hung low as Ray quietly walked out the door. At that moment I turned to the stunned teenagers and said, "Youth, *that* is exactly what Jesus Christ did for you!"

John brought Ray back in and, as you can imagine, it took some time for me to regain control of the classroom.

I simply make the same statement to you decades later, "*That* is exactly what Jesus Christ did for you." The sinless One took your punishment, and while you were still sinning, He died for you!

Through the crucifixion, God showed the world His love. The cross is His Valentine to us. Have you received it?

Listen for the Songbirds
Life Lesson #25

When the doors to the street are closed and the sound of grinding fades; when people rise up at the sound of birds, but all their songs grow faint (Ecclesiastes 12:4).

THIS VERSE REMINDS ME OF MANY MORNINGS DURING the years we lived in the beautiful North Carolina mountains. The first few years we did not have an air-conditioner in the little cabin in the woods where we lived, so I kept the windows open most of the time. The early hues of the first streaks of sunlight accompanied by the sounds of songbirds greeting the day served as our alarm clock. I would lie there and bask in the bliss of the sights, the sounds (including Wayne's sweet sleep sounds), the cool breezes, and the aromas of a new mountain morning.

Then *it* would happen! Crows would fill the trees making loud cawing sounds that (please forgive me if you are a big fan of crows) reminded me of fingernails across a chalkboard. I'd take my pillow and try to cover my ears.

My father had died shortly before we moved to the mountains. Within the first year and a half we lived there, one of my best friends for over forty years and my beloved uncle died two months apart. Then, my mother was diagnosed with terminal cancer. It was a particularly stressful time in my life. I remember one morning lying in bed enjoying the songbirds when the crows flew in and cawed louder than usual. I felt like crying. I even said, "Go away crows, I want to hear the songbirds," and I prayed, "Lord, I *need* to hear the songbirds."

And guess what? As soon as I prayed that prayer, I noticed something remarkable. The songbirds never stopped singing. The sound of the crows overpowered the volume of the songbirds, but they still were singing! From that morning on, I made it a practice to filter out the caws and strain to hear the songs.

That practice became a valuable Life Lesson for me. Each day we are bombarded with negatives—negative news, negative people, negative experiences. However, all these negatives have not chased the positives away! We can learn to filter out the negatives and strain harder to see, hear, and experience the positives.

I believe it's no coincidence the cross is the universal plus sign, the sign that means positive! When we filter the negatives through the power of the cross, the positives prevail.

Solomon was going through a dark time when he wrote the opening scripture. Life had lost its meaning, and all seemed like darkness and vanity. Thankfully, a few verses later we learn he regained his reason for living: *Now all has been heard; here is the conclusion of the matter: Fear God and keep his commandments, for this is the duty of all mankind* (Ecclesiastes 12:13).

Are you going through a time when you desperately need to hear the sound of a songbird, but all you seem to hear is the caw of a crow? Remember, the songs are in the air. Listen hard to hear them. God bless you! Love and prayers.

Go with the Flow
Life Lesson #26

For those who are led by the Spirit of God are the children of God (Romans 8:14).

IF YOU ARE AROUND ME MUCH AT ALL, YOU'VE PROB-ably heard me use the phrase, "Go with the flow." Or, maybe you've heard me say, "That just seems to be going against the flow."

I believe there is a flow to life. When we stay in the flow, life goes more smoothly. I also believe the flow is the presence and guidance of the Holy Spirit.

I learned a very practical lesson about going with the flow when I taught the SYA's (Single Young Adults) Sunday School Class at First Baptist Church of Myrtle Beach. In addition to our Bible study class, we (Lois and all the co-workers who helped with the SYA's) also did local ministries, took mission trips, helped around the church, had a lot of parties, and planned fun activities.

For several years, we took tent camping trips--canoeing, etc. Even though I had a wonderful time, I was a novice in every way, especially when it came to the canoeing. One particular year, I was paired with a young lady, Lynda, who was even more of a novice than I was. We spent the first part of our water adventure going around in circles (literally) because we didn't have our act together with using the oars.

But, then it happened. We began to do things the right way, got into the flow of the downstream, and we had a wonderful excursion.

We were on the river a couple of hours thoroughly enjoying the beautiful day. In fact, we enjoyed it so much, we rowed right past the spot where we were supposed to dock. As we relaxed on the river, we suddenly heard yelling muffled by the river sounds. We looked around and saw our whole group standing in an alcove waving and motioning for us to come back there. The problem was, we were already downstream a good way, and we had to turn the canoe around and paddle back upstream. We had to go against the flow. What a chore it was! We struggled as we fought against the current. Whew! It was much harder than I would have ever imagined, but we made it.

What I learned from this experience:

Going against the flow makes things much more difficult than they need to be!

Going with the flow is much more peaceful than the alternative. Yes, we did have obstacles along that way, too (tree branches, rocks, debris) that slowed us down some, but overall, it was smooth sailing.

Honestly, in your heart, you know what is right and what is wrong. You have a sense of where you should be on the stream of life. If you don't, ask God to show You. He designed a plan for you before He ever created you, and it's not a secret plan. It's one He longs to reveal to you step by step.

The first step is coming into a relationship with Almighty God. He provided the Way, the Truth, and the Life through Jesus Christ! Accepting His forgiveness and grace sets us on the right course.

Let's all pray together that we will walk in faith as we *go with the flow*.

Sweet Aromas
Life Lesson #27

For we are to God the pleasing aroma of Christ among those who are being saved and those who are perishing (2 Corinthians 2:15).

RESEARCHERS SAY SMELL IS ONE THE MOST POWERFUL evokers of memories and the emotions attached to them. Your mother's perfume, your father's pipe, your friend's lip gloss or after-shave can take you back to a certain place in your heart and mind. (Our daughters say the smell of an old calico lounge dress I used to wear on Friday nights for our family nights when they were children has that effect on them.)

What are your favorite smells? Some of mine are: newly mowed grass, fresh rain, smoky wood-burning fireplaces, almost any Italian food, Wayne's tee shirts, the grandchildren when I snuggle them whether they are hot and sweaty from playing or just bathed and dressed in pajamas.

From our opening verse, we see God also has a sense of smell. Let's take a closer look at the smell that most pleases Him.

I cannot imagine how Aaron must have felt the day he became the first High Priest of Israel (Leviticus 8:1-36). Moses publicly cleansed Aaron, probably in the Bronze Laver in the outer court, and dressed him in the ornate attire prepared for the High Priest. He then poured special anointing oil on Aaron's head. According to David, in Psalm 133:2, the oil ran from Aaron's head, down to his beard, and onto the collar of his robe. The aroma of the anointing oil signaled the people the High Priest would soon be ready to present the sacrifices. Aaron had seven additional days of ordination beyond the day of his cleansing ritual before his priestly duties began. The sweet aroma of the anointing oil lingered on his head, his beard, and his clothing during that time.

We are told in Hebrews 4:14-16 Jesus is our High Priest. As the great High Priest, Jesus didn't just offer a sacrifice as Aaron had, He *became* the sacrifice that would atone for the sins of the world! As I thought about this, I wondered if Jesus experienced an ordination similar to Aaron.

His baptism by John fulfilled the public cleansing required by a priest (Matthew 3:13-14). Also, in the narrative of the days leading up to Jesus's crucifixion, the Bible tells of two acts of honor performed by a woman (some commentators believe it was two different women) identified as "a sinner" in Luke, and as Mary in other gospels (Matthew 26:6-13; Mark 14:3-9; Luke 7:36-50; John 12:1-8). As Jesus was eating in the home of Simon, the woman stood behind Him weeping. She cried so hard, her tears covered His feet. Then she wiped her tears from His feet with her hair. In a real sense, that was also a public cleansing.

In the other account, Mary broke open an alabaster container of costly perfume and poured on His head. The perfume/oil flowed from His head, to His beard, and onto His clothes. Jesus said she had anointed Him for his burial (John 12:7; Matthew 26:12). The events of Holy Week happened so quickly, Jesus probably kept the aroma on Him from that moment—through His betrayal, His trial, His beating, and even through His death. Praise God for the sweet aroma that reminded Him of the love of His follower(s)!

So, in a real sense with the cleansing and anointing, Jesus was ordained as the High Priest in much the same way as Aaron. How about us? The scripture tells us when we are born again into the family of God, we become priests. Do we go through a similar ordination as Aaron and Jesus?

Yes, we do! Our cleansing is through the blood of Jesus, and our anointing is through the Holy Spirit. Then, and only then, can we be the *pleasing aroma of Christ* to God!

As priests, what sacrifices can we offer to God this side of the cross? According to scripture, our sacrifices are:

- **A contrite heart – (Psalm 51:17)**
- **Our bodies as living sacrifices – (Romans 12:1)**
- **Our praise and the fruit of our lips openly professing our faith – (Hebrews 13:15)**
- **Doing good and sharing with others – (Hebrews 13:16)**

I pray we may leave the sweet aroma of Christ, pleasing to God, everywhere we go! My prayer is in Jesus' name.

Betrayed

Life Lesson #28

Then Judas Iscariot, one of the Twelve, went to the chief priests to betray Jesus to them. They were delighted to hear this and promised to give him money. So he watched for an opportunity to hand him over (Mark 14:10-11).

SEVERAL OF US WERE ASKED TO DO A MORNING devotional on a local radio station. My week fell during Holy Week, so I decided to include some of the experiences Jesus encountered during His last week before the crucifixion.

I started work on a devotional about "betrayal," and I must admit I was quite moved by the meaning and depth of it all. In the process of preparing it, I realized betrayal causes some of the deepest hurt a human can experience. The more I thought about it, the more I realized there are reasons betrayal is such a hurtful experience.

Betrayal causes grief. It's not just grief based on one loss, it is multi-dimensional. Betrayal is made up of many layers of grief caused by accumulated losses. The following are just a few you may have experienced and found to be true.

First, and probably most obviously, betrayal causes the loss of trust. Once our trust in a person is broken, it is very difficult to regain it (even if it should be regained.) Wayne often says, "Forgiveness is a gift, but trust is earned." Sometimes people do repent and desire to be trusted again. Simon Peter, who denied Jesus three times, repented and became one of the greatest evangelizers of the first century. Even Judas regretted betraying Jesus and tried to give back the blood money, admitting he had betrayed the Innocent One (Matthew 27:3-4).

However, others make a lifetime practice of betrayal. Time, circumstances, and--most importantly--the Holy Spirit will help us discern if we should ever again trust the one who betrayed us.

Secondly, betrayal not only leads to the loss of trust, but also the loss of a dream. If you had a close relationship with the person who betrayed you, you probably pictured that relationship remaining forever. You envisioned happy times that would lead to happy memories. Losing a relationship is always hard. Losing a relationship through betrayal is even harder. Once again, forgive the person, but seek God's guidance concerning whether or not you should trust him or her again.

Thirdly, betrayal often leads to the loss of tangible things like money, a job, other friends/ relationships, and maybe even family members. The grief that accompanies these types of losses is difficult because the repercussions take time to heal and overcome.

Lastly, betrayal often causes grief because it is humiliating to the betrayed person. Betrayals tend to be public and can be very embarrassing. Being demeaned in the eyes of others carries its own kind of grief.

So what can we do about it? How can we deal with betrayal?

As mentioned above, forgiveness is not just an option, it is a necessity. The longer we hold onto un-forgiveness, the longer we allow the betrayer to have control over us. For our sakes, for their sakes, but most of all for the sake of obeying God, we must forgive.

Also, we need to realize a person who hurts or betrays another person, is really a hurting person himself/herself. I read a statement years ago that was life-changing for me, and I really do believe it is true: "People don't do things *against* you, they do things *for* themselves."

If a personal betrayal comes to your mind, try to see how the above statement is true and applicable in the life of the betrayer.

Most importantly, as we are in this Holy Season leading up to the commemoration of the death, burial, and resurrection of our Lord, let's think about the ways Jesus was betrayed while on earth, and how He reacted in the face of betrayal. From the religious leaders, to some of His family members, and even to His own followers, He was betrayed often and for wrong reasons. Still, from the cross, He prayed, '*Father, forgive them, for they do not know what they are doing*' (Luke 23:34).

Hallelujah, what a Savior! And what an example for us all.

THE CUP
LIFE LESSON #29

Then he said to them, 'My soul is overwhelmed with sorrow to the point of death. Stay here and keep watch with me.' Going a little farther, he fell with his face to the ground and prayed, 'My Father, if it is possible, may this cup be taken from me. Yet not as I will, but as you will' (Matthew 26:38-39).

THE ABOVE VERSE BREAKS MY HEART AS I THINK OF Jesus feeling overwhelmed with sorrow. Have you ever experienced sorrow so deep you felt as though you might literally die? If so, that depth of sorrow is what our precious Savior experienced in Gethsemane after the Passover meal with His disciples.

If we continue reading this passage through verse 45, we see He prayed three times for "this cup" to be taken from Him. And three times He surrendered to the Father's will.

Several years ago as I read this passage, I had a strong feeling there was much more to the cup than I realized. I began researching, and I asked many different people their opinion of what the cup represented. Most people said Jesus did not want to suffer and die, and that was the cup. I feel sure that thought is partially true, but I sensed there was something more we had overlooked that made His struggle so difficult. After all, He knew He was going to die. He even tried to warn His followers of His impending death.

So, I searched through the Bible for passages that spoke of any kind of cup. Then I began to put the pieces together as I saw what I believe is the bigger picture of the cup Jesus struggled with as He prayed in Gethsemane.

"The cup" is a Hebrew idiom that refers to any experience--good or bad--that completely engulfs a person. I noticed in scripture two types of cups, one type was wonderful, the other was terrible. One was the cup of joy, and the other was the cup of affliction.

The cups of joy are salvation (Psalm 116:13), consolation (Jeremiah 16:7), and blessing (I Corinthians 10:16 KJV). The cups of affliction are the fury of God's wrath poured out on sin (Jeremiah 25:15), the cup of scorn and derision (Ezekiel 23:32), ruin and desolation (Ezekiel 23:33), trembling and fury (Isaiah 51:17, 22), and God's judgment (Revelation 14:10).

I believe the cup Jesus referred to in His prayer was, most of all, the fury of God's wrath poured out on the judgment of sin. He, who was well-pleasing to the Father, would feel the wrath and fury that accompanies the judgment of sin.

What I am about to say is one of the most important things I will ever write: God doesn't *excuse* sin, He *judges* it. The judgment of sin is death. But, in the greatest act of mercy known to mankind, Jesus--God in the flesh--bore the judgment of our sin. In a mystery we cannot explain because it's divine, He took on our sin, and He died in our place.

God made him who had no sin to be sin for us, so that in him we might become the righteousness of God (2 Corinthians 5:21).

Do you see how amazing this is? He drank from the cup of affliction so we could drink the cup of joy! No good works on our part could ever pay the penalty for our sin.

I believe we get so used to saying, "Jesus died for our sins," we fail to realize the depth of what that really means. I want you to think of the most despicable sin you can imagine--one so horrific just thinking of it makes you uneasy. What if the only way you could have a relationship with the person you love the most was to commit that sin? Could you do it? Then bring into your mind and heart the realization that on the cross, the sinless One, Jesus, took on that despicable sin and every other sin imaginable. No wonder Jesus struggled with drinking from *the cup*!

Why did He do it? Because He loves us so much He longs for a relationship with us, but our sin separates us from Him. So, He took the judgment for our sin, and He shared His righteousness with us. He provided the only way we could ever come into a relationship with holy God!

If you are a believer, you drink from the cup of joy because Jesus drank from the cup of affliction for you. If you have not yet done so, please let today be *your* day of salvation.

The Cup (Part 2)
Life Lesson #30

I tell you, I will not drink from this fruit of the vine from now on until that day when I drink it new with you in my Father's kingdom (Matthew 26:29).

I HAVE BEEN SO EXCITED ABOUT THIS LIFE LESSON because God showed me a beautiful picture of His love through it. I hope the same will be true for you.

The biblical wedding customs consisted of three main parts: the betrothal, the wedding, the consummation. The betrothal was similar to engagement today except that it was legally binding. However, the couple could not be together--or even be in each other's presence--until after the wedding ceremony (which was usually around a year later.)

The Betrothal:

The father of the groom chose the bride for his son. God the Father chose you as the bride for His Son (Revelation 21:9).

When the time was right, the father and his son met with the prospective bride and her father with two witnesses present. The bridegroom read a contract of the ways he would love and care for his bride. Our Bridegroom gave us beautiful promises in scripture (2 Corinthians 1:20).

The bridegroom then presented the bride price, similar to a dowry, to the bride's father. Our Heavenly Bridegroom paid our bride price with His own blood (I Peter 1:18, 19).

The Bridegroom poured the cup of wine and drank from it. If the prospective bride accepted the proposal, she also drank from the cup. Their next cup of wine together would be at their wedding ceremony (Matthew 26:29).

Then, the bridegroom presented gifts to the bride to help her prepare for the wedding. Our Bridegroom gave us spiritual gifts to help us prepare for His coming (1 Corinthians 7:7).

As the bridegroom left his future bride, he promised her he was going to prepare the bridal chamber at his father's house, and one day he would return to take her home with him. Reflect on Jesus' precious promises (John 14:1-4).

After the future groom left, the bride wore a veil in public as a sign she was set apart for her groom. Her responsibility in the relationship was to look forward to, and prepare for, the day he would come for her. She was to remain pure as she waited for her groom (Revelation 19:7-8).

The Wedding:

Only the father of the groom knew when the wedding date would be. He made his decision based on the progress of the bridal chamber. Only the heavenly Father knows when our Bridegroom will come for us (Matthew 24:36).

When the bridal chamber was ready, the father told his son to go and get his bride. The groom awakened his best man (called "the friend of the bridegroom" in scripture) who ran through the village shouting and blowing a shofar trumpet announcing the bridegroom was coming. (I Thessalonians 4:16 tells us that there will be a shout and a trumpet sound as our Bridegroom comes for us. Also see Matthew 25:6).

The groom waited outside the bride's home as she came out to meet him. They, and all the awakened villagers, processed to the wedding site. Once again the bridegroom and bride shared a cup of wine at the end of the ceremony (Matthew 26:29).

The Consummation:

This custom may seem strange to the western mind, but when the newlyweds entered the bridal chamber as a couple, the *friend of the bridegroom* waited outside the door. After the marriage was consummated, the groom told his friend. The friend then announced it to the waiting guests who rejoiced because the couple had entered into blood covenant (John 3:29).

The guests celebrated while the couple remained inside the bridal chamber. When the newlyweds emerged (usually a week later), the marriage supper--a big party--took place. (Perhaps we can better understand why the host of the wedding party, in the story of Jesus' water to wine miracle, ran out of wine by the time the big party took place.)

Do you see how much of what Jesus said in scripture, and how much of what Paul wrote, were "wedding talk?" I believe everything God does is in preparation for the day we will live in His presence eternally.

As we saw in the last Life Lesson, two kinds of cups are found in scripture--one of affliction and one of joy. Our Bridegroom drank the cup of affliction. He offers us the cup of joy. Will you accept His proposal?

Since I learned this Life Lesson, each time I drink from the cup at communion, I realize anew its meaning. Through it, I reaffirm my betrothal to my heavenly Bridegroom. I wrote the following poem to express my gratitude for the price He paid - for you - for me.

The cup that we share is far from the same,
Mine smells of joy, while His reeks of shame.
My portion is wholesome, but His so much worse,
For mine is a blessing, while His was a curse.
The cup shows God's love, its depth and its breadth,
My part brings new life, but His brought cruel death.
And so, as our lips touch the cup in a pledge,
I taste the sweet juice, while He drinks the dregs.

Famous Last Words
Life Lesson #31

This week has been quite emotional for me as I considered Jesus' words from the cross. I pray I can convey the beauty contained in this Life Lesson through looking at the sayings in context.

"The Seven Last Words"

1. The Roman guards were accustomed to being cursed and insulted by those who were crucified. In fact, they expected it. What they did not expect was Jesus of Nazareth looking down from the cross and praying, *'Father, forgive them, for they do not know what they are doing'* (Luke 23:34). I wonder if this could have been the first event that led to the Roman centurion's conversion?

2. Often those being crucified called out to their gods and asked for horrible retribution to befall their executioners. On one side of Jesus, a thief mocked His claim of Divinity. On the other side, a thief recognized Him as Messiah and asked to enter His Kingdom. Jesus assured the new believer, *'Today you will be with me in Paradise'* (Luke 23:43).

3. At a certain point in crucifixions, the closest family members and friends of the victims were allowed to come within a specific proximity of the crosses to say goodbye. We don't know who all came to Jesus' cross, but we know His mother, Mary, and His disciple, John, were there. Jesus told Mary, *'Woman* [in that culture a term of respect similar to "lady" or "ma'am"] *this is your son.'* Then He told John, *'This is your mother.'* Even in His pain and agony, Jesus was concerned about His mother (John 19:26).

   At noon, darkness covered the whole land until three in the afternoon (Mark 15:33). This darkness was supernatural, for there was no natural reason. Passover (the day Jesus died) always falls on a full moon, and solar eclipses don't occur on full moons.

In scripture, light symbolizes God, and darkness symbolizes the opposite (sin.) Darkness also symbolizes God's judgment. In Exodus 10:21-23, darkness covered the land of Egypt because they defied God. The scripture says it was so dark, the darkness could be felt. I believe the same could be said about the darkness during the crucifixion.

4. When the darkness dispelled, and *at about three in the afternoon Jesus cried in a loud voice, 'My God, My God, why have you forsaken me'* (**Matthew 27:46**)?
   Many Bible scholars believe the sin Jesus bore for you and me made Him feel separated from holy God. He felt as though God had forsaken Him, and He quoted David's prayer from Psalm 22:1.
   Several researchers took the key words of that question in Greek and applied the other definition for "why" (which can be a statement rather than a question) and "forsake" (which can mean "leave in a place" rather than "abandon.") They believe Jesus may have exclaimed in a loud voice, "My God, My God, [this is] why You left me here!" In their explanation, they feel it was a victory cry as He acknowledged He had become the redemption for mankind.

   Either way, it is a powerful saying.

5. *Later, knowing that everything had now been finished, and so that Scripture would be fulfilled, Jesus said, 'I am thirsty'* (John 19:28). Jesus was thirsty. His dehydration started in the Garden of Gethsemane when He prayed passionately to escape the cup. His perspiration became blood. The beating and scourging resulted in further blood loss, and the combination of perspiration and bleeding on the cross left Him in a state of acute dehydration. He was thirsty.

I also wonder if His request could have been for more than liquid relief. In the above verse, *thirst* can also mean "to earnestly desire." Could it be He longed to spare His Bride from the darkness He had just experienced? Could the cup He had prayed so fervently to escape have now become His earnest desire for the sake of His Bride?

6. *'It is finished'* (John 19:30). The spotless Lamb of God fulfilled scripture and died for the sins of the world. He had done all that was required. "Jesus Paid It All!"

7. ***Jesus called out with a loud voice, 'Father, into your hands I commit my spirit'*** (Luke 23:46). The first prayer I learned was a bedtime prayer: "Now I lay me down to sleep, I pray Thee, Lord, my soul to keep. If I should die before I wake, I pray Thee, Lord, my soul to take."

Jewish mothers taught their children to recite the following scripture verse, as their first learned prayer, at night before bed: *'Into Your hands I commit my spirit; You have redeemed me, O Lord God of truth'* (Psalm 31:5). Quite possibly, Jesus' first prayer was also His last!

This Life Lesson caused me to ponder what I would like my final words to be. I asked my husband, Wayne, the same question. He thought for a moment and said, "Thank you." I exclaimed, "Those are my words, too!" Although there's much more we could say, "Thank you" seems to sum it up.

I want to say "thank you" to you as readers for taking this journey to Calvary with me these past few Life Lessons. I'd also like to say it one more time, "Hallelujah, what a Savior!"

Because He Lives
Life Lesson #32

JESUS' LIFELESS BODY WAS TAKEN FROM THE CROSS and quickly prepared for burial before Passover sunset. He was placed in a freshly hewn tomb which belonged to Joseph of Arimathea. Isn't it amazing Jesus was born in a borrowed stable and buried in a borrowed tomb?

The religious leaders convinced Pilate to seal the tomb so none of Jesus' followers could steal His body and claim He rose from the dead as He had prophesied. Historians say in sealing a tomb, a ball of hot wax was placed on each side of the tomb entrance affixing the ends of a special piece of material stretched across the stone placed in front of the tomb's entrance. Pilate's signet ring imprinted his symbol on each ball of wax which flattened it and proved he ordered the sealing.

Pilate even ordered Roman soldiers to guard the tomb around the clock. Every man-made precaution was put in place to insure Jesus' body stayed in the tomb.

However, man-made precautions could not keep Jesus in the tomb. Praise God! In three days the stone supernaturally rolled away, and Jesus walked out of the tomb resurrected, alive, and alive forevermore!

Numbers of people saw Jesus after the resurrection: those who came to the tomb, two men on the road to Emmaus, the disciples gathered together in a room and later joined by Thomas, a group of five hundred people, and followers on the mount of the ascension. His resurrection is well-documented in secular writings and in scripture.

The resurrection was a central point in history. But now, after over two thousand years, the question we each must face is, "What does the resurrection mean to you, to me?" Although there are glorious aspects too numerous to cover in one Life Lesson, I would like to share a few facets of the resurrection that mean the most to me.

Because He lives…
Jesus overcame death. *The wages of sin is death, but the gift of God is eternal life in Christ Jesus our Lord* (Romans 6:23). On the cross, Jesus took the punishment of death caused by our sin, and at the resurrection He proved His

power triumphs over death. Even though our bodies will cease to function, our souls (the essence of who we are) and our Spirits will never die.

Because He lives...
Jesus defeated the enemy. Do you realize what that means to us? Satan can't bully us. If we have a relationship with the Son of God, the works of the enemy have been destroyed! *The one who practices sin is of the devil; for the devil has sinned from the beginning. The Son of God appeared for this purpose, to destroy the works of the devil* (I John 3:8).

Because He lives...
Jesus' resurrection set the precedent that we will rise again like Him. *But Christ has indeed been raised from the dead, the first-fruits of those who have fallen asleep* (I Corinthians 15:20).

Because He lives...
Jesus opened the way for us to experience the power of the Holy Spirit. The same power that brought Jesus out of the grave indwells His followers: *And if the Spirit of him who raised Jesus from the dead is living in you, he who raised Christ from the dead will also give life to your mortal bodies because of his Spirit who lives in you* (Romans 8:11).

It blesses me beyond measure to think His resurrection power lives in me! In the book, Unscripted, Jeff Iorg points out when we become believers we are baptized by the Holy Spirit and receive the initial filling of the Spirit (I Corinthians 12:13); we are given Spiritual gifts (I Corinthians 7:7); we are sealed with the Holy Spirit (Ephesians 1:13); we are made a member of the global church (Ephesians 3:10-12); and we become a part of the body of Christ (I Corinthians 12:12-27). Wow! All of this because He lives!

Jesus overcame death, destroyed the works of the devil, and paved the way for us to experience resurrection. He even gives us dynamic power to live each day. What more could we ever desire?

So I ask you again, "What does the resurrection mean to you?" Please consider this question anew today.

I hope the words of the old hymn will be especially meaningful to you at this time: "He arose! He arose! Hallelujah, Christ arose!"

Out of Sight, But Not Out of Mind
Life Lesson #33

Please read: Acts 1:6-11

The date was Resurrection Day, April 14 of 1968. I was a senior at Limestone College in Gaffney, South Carolina, and Wayne was a student at Southeastern Seminary in Wake Forest, North Carolina. After church that Sunday night, when Wayne took me home, my parents and sister, Lynn, were already asleep. So, the two of us knelt at the coffee table in the living room and had our own special communion service with grape juice and crackers.

Afterwards, Wayne handed me a beautifully wrapped gift and said he almost gave it to me the night before so I could wear it with my Easter dress. I thought maybe it was a decorative pin, but when I opened it, I saw a sparkling engagement ring! I gasped, "I don't know what to do!" to which Wayne replied, "I don't, either."

Then I asked, "But what about the butterfly?" Wayne's expression showed me he had no idea what I meant. So, I reminded him how when we were teenagers, a group of us were sitting on the car hoods at a local drive-in restaurant discussing the that a high school couple had just gotten engaged. I remembered Wayne saying, "I think that would be like taking a little butterfly and clipping its wings." I also remembered me thinking, "That boy will never get married."

Wayne laughed when I reminded him about what he had said, and he replied, "That was before I fell in love with you." (It still brings tears to my eyes.) Then he knelt on one knee and asked me to marry him. I gladly accepted, and the second greatest journey of my life began. (The first was when I accepted Jesus as my Savior.)

The day after the engagement, we had fun calling friends and sharing the news. But then, Wayne had to return to seminary, and we we would not see each other for several weeks. However, even though he was out of my sight, he was not out of my mind. From that point on, my thoughts, my plans, my love were focused on preparing for the day we would become husband and wife.

After the resurrection, Jesus remained on earth for forty days. He continued teaching His disciples and communing with them at different times. Sometimes He met them at a "mountain in Galilee." However, in today's scripture, Jesus had arranged to meet with His followers one final time on the Mount of Olives near Jerusalem.

They immediately began asking Him more questions about the coming Kingdom. He assured them only The Father in Heaven knows exactly when it will happen, but He gave them very specific instructions as to what they were to do in the meantime. They were to focus their lives on telling others about Him: *'But you will receive power when the Holy Spirit comes on you; and you will be my witnesses in Jerusalem, and in all Judea and Samaria, and to the ends of the earth'* (Acts 1:8).

In Jesus' day, if a rabbi had a new teaching or a clarification of some Hebrew scriptures, he was required to present his ideas to the religious leaders and to the world at large. However, if He died before His teachings were accepted, his followers would become his "living witnesses" who would prove to the world their rabbi's teachings were true.

Do you see the amazing calling Jesus entrusted to His disciples (down through the centuries) to be His witnesses? We are to show the world His teachings--love God, love others--are the true meaning of life.

Immediately after Jesus gave them this commission, He was taken up into the clouds, and they could see Him no longer. They looked intently into the sky as He was going, when suddenly two men dressed in white stood beside them: *'Men of Galilee,' they said, 'why do you stand here looking into the sky? This same Jesus, who has been taken from you into heaven, will come back in the same way you have seen him go into heaven'* (Acts 1:10-11).

He then was out of their sights, but He was not to be out of their minds. The same should be true for us today. We should focus our thoughts, our plans, our love on preparing for the day He comes for us!

Wayne should be getting home in a few minutes. Even after 49 years of marriage, I still get a quickening in my heart when I hear his footsteps approaching the door. With his schedule and my schedule, he hasn't been in my sight the whole day, but he has definitely been in my mind.

Likewise, the signs of the times confirm our Bridegroom will be coming soon. Can you imagine the quickening our hearts will feel when we hear Him approaching? Yes, He is out of sight--for now--but we cannot let Him be out of mind! After all, we are His *living witnesses*!

The Language of Love
Life Lesson #34

*If I speak with the tongues of men and of angels, but have
not love, I am like a resounding gong or a clanging cymbal* (I
Corinthians 13:1).

HOW IS IT THAT TWO PEOPLE WHO TRULY LOVE
each other can have an emotional disconnect when it comes to sharing and
receiving love? As a minister's wife, and generally in life, I've seen many
marriages and/or relationships injured because one or the other did not
feel they were loved. Yet, I knew they loved each other. I could see it, but
oftentimes, they couldn't.

Several years ago I attended a conference at the LifeWay Conference
Center in Ridgecrest, North Carolina, to scout out some of the new disci-
pleship courses being offered to churches. One night the evening worship
speaker was Dr. Gary Chapman who presented his then new book entitled,
The Five Love Languages. That was it!

Everything he presented made so much sense I called our Minister of
Education the next morning and asked for permission to buy the disciple-
ship program to bring home to the church. I remember telling him the
things Dr. Chapman presented could help save marriages--and they have.

Basically, Dr. Chapman teaches we each have a dominant love language
we *speak*. It is how we best give and receive love. The problem is in relationships often the people involved speak different love languages, and the emotional needs of each go unmet. (Of course, no one person can meet all the
emotional needs of another.)

The five "Love Languages" are the following:

Gift giving
Quality time
Words of affection
Acts of service
Physical touch

First determine which of these is the way you are most comfortable giving love, and the way you feel most loved. Then, try to determine the love language of others, and learn to *speak* their language as you help them understand yours.

As I reflected on the love languages, I realized Jesus spoke all five of them.

1. He constantly gave gifts--eternal life, healing, new beginnings.
2. He carved out quality time with His followers to teach and encourage them. If the crowds pressed on them too hard, He gathered them in a boat and launched out into the sea to spend time with them.
3. He spoke words of affection often referring to His great love for His friends. He spoke life and love to those around Him. Can you imagine how the adulterous woman must have felt when she heard, '*Then neither do I condemn you...go now and leave your life of sin*' (John 8:11 NIV)?
4. He performed acts of service ranging from changing water into wine for a wedding host to feeding 5,000 hungry people on a hillside.
5. His physical touches were transformational as He often healed people through touching them.

I woke up early this morning. I did not feel quite rested enough, so I went back to bed for awhile and thought about what I would write in this Life Lesson. Suddenly, a thought entered my mind that filled my heart with awe and worship: Jesus spoke all five love languages from the cross!

Please let me explain what I mean.

Gift giving--He offered eternal life to the repentant thief.
Quality time--He hung on the cross for six hours to redeem us.
Words of affection--He spoke forgiveness to the ones who were murdering Him.
Acts of service--He entrusted His precious mother into the hands of His beloved disciple, John.
Physical touch--please stay with me on this one because it absolutely blows me away. We know Jesus could not physically touch or hug anyone while He was on the cross because His arms were stretched across the rough, splintery wood, and His hands were nailed to the cross. *But...*

A study I did several years ago prompted questions in my mind, and I sought answers to those questions. I went to a trusted orthopedic surgeon for his counsel. I asked him about the effect of a nail (about the size of a railroad spike) going through the indention in the wrist which was considered part of the hand.

I specifically asked if that injury would cause the middle finger and the ring finger to bend toward the palm leaving the other fingers somewhat straight. He pondered this for a long time. Then he said, "Yes, Joy. You're exactly right." He explained the carpal tunnel-type effect that would have resulted, and he gave the medical reasons why.

With tears in my eyes I replied, "Then, Dr. Ward, that means on the cross Jesus' hands formed the letters of what has become the international sign for 'I Love You!'"

Do you see how beautiful this is? Jesus used His hands the only way He could while nailed to a cross to express "I Love You" one final time. When I think of His great love, I wish I could coin a special *Language of Love* to tell the world how wonderful our Savior is!

Brokenness
Life Lesson #35

Now as they were eating, Jesus took bread, and after blessing it broke it and gave it to the disciples, and said, 'Take, eat; this is my body' (Matthew 26:26 ESV).

THIS VERSE IS SPECIAL TO ME. ONE THANKSGIVING Eve, Wayne spiked a high fever and asked me to fill in for him that night at the Wednesday night church service. As I quickly searched for verses on giving thanks, I found Matthew 26:26, and four phrases immediately caught my attention.

When I read our focal verse that Wednesday night, I realized Matthew 26:26 is essentially a microcosm of the Christian life. I was amazed! This one verse contains an understanding of what happens to us from conversion (accepting Jesus as our Savior) until death.

The four phrases are the following: He took; He blessed ("gave thanks" in some translations); He broke; He gave. Please remember this nugget of truth: A direct correlation exists between what God does in the natural, and what He does in the spiritual. We can see that principle throughout scripture.

On a very basic, natural level, Matthew 26:26 is about Jesus passing out the bread at the Passover Meal/Seder. However, it also shows what Jesus does in the life of each believer. The spiritual application is what we will consider in this Life Lesson.

He took:
When I looked up the definitions for *took* in Greek (Strong's Concordance), I could have shouted. Here are but a few of the definitions: "to take with the hand; lay hold of any person or thing in order to use it; to take to one's self; to give access to one's self; that which is taken is not let go; to associate one's self as companion."

Such beauty! When Jesus takes us, He takes us to Himself, He makes us His own, He associates Himself as our companion, He will not let us go.

So, the question arises, "Whom does Jesus *take*?" I believe it's anyone who will let Him:

Everyone who calls on the name of the Lord will be saved (Romans 10:13).

He is patient with you, not wanting anyone to perish, but everyone to come into repentance (2 Peter 3:9).

For God loved the world so much that he gave his one and only son, that whoever believes in him shall not perish but have eternal life (John 3:16).

He blessed:
In the Greek dictionary, if *bless* refers to God doing the blessing, it means "to cause to prosper; to make happy; to bestow blessings on; favored of God; blessed."

He broke:
Broke in Greek simply means "broke." We'll see more on that later.

He gave:
Some of the Greek definitions for *gave* include: "of one's own accord to give one something; to commission; to reach out, extend, commit."

Jesus takes us, He blesses us, sometimes He has to break us to help us become capable of receiving more blessings, He gives of Himself to us, and He commissions us to give to others. A picture of life is painted in a few short words!

Please notice this important detail: Jesus held the bread in His hand the entire time. Once He took it, He never let it go until it fulfilled its intended purpose (to be eaten).

Likewise, Jesus hold us in His hand throughout life. He never lets us go. When we have completed our intended purpose on earth, He then resides with us in Heaven.

Because brokenness is such an important subject, we will have a part 2 to this Life Lesson. Until then, please remember the following:

1. **Brokenness hurts.** I know. I've been there. But brokenness doesn't last forever. God wants us to be made whole, so He helps heal the brokenness.

2. **Brokenness serves a purpose.** Sometimes brokenness is the only way we can become what we were created to be. Also, it makes us more sensitive to the needs of others, and we can help them in their brokenness.

In a novel I'm writing, the leading man asks his best friend the following: "Gil, do you think one human can...can heal...another human?"

"Whoa," Gil responded as he quickly swallowed his mouthful of coffee. "That's one for the theologians! Why do you ask?"

Bob looked past him with a contemplative stare. "Because ever since Sarah came into my life, it seems pieces of my heart I didn't even know were broken have been healed."

Gil nodded. "I see. Well, she certainly loves God, and I admire that. Maybe He just gives her some of His extra love to fix you. You've sure got enough that needs fixing," Gil said jokingly.

"Spoken like a true best friend," Bob laughed as he reached for his ringing cell phone.

If you feel you are in a place of brokenness right now, remember "this too shall pass." Instead of fighting it, ask God to show you what you can learn through it. It always serves a purpose.

Brokenness (Part 2)
Life Lesson #36

...to bestow on them a crown of beauty instead of ashes, the oil of joy instead of mourning and a garment of praise instead of a spirit of despair...(Isaiah 61:3).

WHAT DO MOSAICS, STAINED GLASS ART, KALEIDO-scopes, and kintsugi have in common? They are all made of broken pieces (or at least they originally were.) The broken pieces, placed in the right places, make them more beautiful and more valuable.

Have you ever thought about that truth before? Brokenness leads to strength and beauty! In our focal verse, God assures us when He heals brokenness, beauty comes from sadness, joy from mourning, and praise from despair. What a powerful realization!

I'd like to share a few things I've learned about brokenness in my lifetime. I hope these observations will help you in some way. If you are going through a time of brokenness right now, my prayers are with you.

1. **We're all broken at various times in our lives.**
   I love the quote which seems to be a combination of a quote by Ernest Hemingway and the lines of a song by composer Leonard Cohen:

   "We're all broken. That's how the light gets in."

   How true! When we're broken, we look for the Light more than when we are whole.

2. **Most people try to hide their brokenness.**
   Healing may not happen unless we admit the need for healing. Admitting brokenness is difficult because most people want to appear to be self-sufficient. My husband, Wayne, says, "admitting a problem is 50% of solving it." Admitting our brokenness sets us on the path to healing.

3. **Some people may not realize they are broken.**
    When people have lived in dysfunction for a long time (some people their entire lives), they may not realize they are not living the whole life available to them through God's mercy and grace.

4. **We may not recognize the places we are broken.**
    Often we place the blame on obvious issues in our lives when the brokenness runs much deeper. Allowing the Holy Spirit to spotlight the areas of brokenness can help us bring them to God for healing.

5. **Brokenness serves a purpose if we will allow it to do so.**
    We tend to think of brokenness as a terrible thing to be avoided at all costs. People fill their lives with things (and other people) to help them feel whole for even a little while. However, brokenness serves a purpose we can see only in retrospect.

6. **Don't let your brokenness cut other people; they're broken, too.**
    It's a terrible feeling to reach into a sink of dishes and cut your finger on a dish you did not realize was broken. It's likewise a terrible thing to be cut to the core by a person who is broken. Watch out for the broken pieces of others. "Hurting people hurt people." Try not to let yourself be one of those who hurts and/or is hurt.

7. **Brokenness won't last forever, unless we choose to wallow in the self-pity that often accompanies it.**
    Some people call attention to themselves by calling attention to their brokenness. If you do this, you will stay in a rut that will prevent you from moving from brokenness to wholeness. Accept what has happened as a part of life, and don't spend your life dwelling on the past.

8. **You are more valuable once you've experienced brokenness.**
    Please re-read Isaiah 61:3. *Beauty*, *joy*, and *praise* emerge at a level that cannot fully be understood apart from *ashes*, *mourning*, and *despair*. The benefits far outweigh the brokenness.

Legend has it a leader was not pleased with the job Chinese craftsmen had done repairing his broken ceramic bowl. He hired Japanese craftsmen to find a more beautiful way to mend broken ceramic dishes.

They developed kintsugi which uses a strong adhesive to put the pieces back together, and sprinkles gold dust on the seams. So rather than trying to hide the flaws, they highlight them with gold dust. Not only are the gold-laced ceramic pieces more beautiful than they were before they were mended, but also they are stronger because of the strong adhesive used to fix them. Kintsugi pieces are much more valuable than unbroken ceramic pieces.

Have you ever thought your times of brokenness can make you more valuable? The lessons you learn, the identity with and sensitivity to the needs of others you develop, the closeness you feel to God when you need Him more than ever, and the healing you experience during times of brokenness do, indeed, make you more valuable.

I saw a Facebook post I liked, although I cannot verify the source. It read, "Some day someone will hug you so tight, it will glue all your broken pieces back together."

Won't you let God do that for you now? His love is the source of all healing. He knows how brokenness can end up being one of the greatest blessings of your life. He provides the results--*beauty*, *joy*, and *praise*.

On Potential
Life Lesson #37

...The LORD does not look at the things people look at. People look at the outward appearance, but the LORD looks at the heart (I Samuel 16:7).

I'M VERY GRATEFUL FOR TODAY'S FOCAL VERSE. ON the days I know I'm not at my best, this verse assures me God looks beyond *me* to what He's placed inside me.

I love to look for the potential in people and situations, and rarely am I disappointed. If I am, it's usually because I give up the search too soon.

When our daughters, Meri Beth and Molly, were in high school, their chorus teacher unexpectedly quit his job. Even though I am not a choral director, I knew chorus just met the first three periods of the day and there were only two months of school left, so I figured I could handle being the substitute for the remainder of the school year. The principal excitedly agreed when I volunteered to help. (I soon found out why he so readily agreed.)

It was a fun little job that first week. We did musical activities and sang some. Then toward the end of the week I decided I should clean out the former teacher's messy office before the new teacher came in the fall. As I sorted and threw away papers, my eyes fell on the words that shook me to the core of my being. This chorus was scheduled to sing at 7:00 am at a hotel for the State Dental Association's annual meeting...in two weeks!

I called the number on the letter hoping they would say it was a mistake, but they didn't. The next day I asked the students if they knew anything about it, but they didn't. I asked if they had anything prepared for it, but they didn't. I went to the principal and begged him to let me cancel, but he didn't. That's when I found out the chorus was also scheduled to perform in a school assembly program and for the community. No wonder the teacher quit! So...

I told the classes, "It will take a miracle, but I do believe in miracles, and it can only happen if we all work together." They told me about a little musical they had sung through twice, so I got it out of the file, and we began working on it.

Because I didn't know anything about the students, I gave the male lead to a boy who was considered a "juvenile delinquent," the female lead to a girl who froze up when she stood before her peers, and the main speaking part to a boy with dyslexia. Also, I put a boy in charge of sound who would walk out of situations if he got too stressed.

Students began volunteering to help with choreography, the designing of T-shirts, and building the set. It was happening, and it was a beautiful thing to behold as it became *their* program.

The big day arrived, and I drove to the school about 6:00 am to check on the bus drivers. I sat in my car and started laughing as I realized the only two students I knew for sure would show up were our own daughters. Then, by the carloads they arrived, and the first time I ever led a choir was in front of 500 dentists in a hotel ballroom. The students were magnificent! Afterwards, we went out for breakfast before returning to school, and we rocked that pancake house with excitement.

However, an interesting thing happened when we presented the program at the school. At first, they were extremely nervous in front of the people who knew them---their peers. The female lead tried to sing, but nothing came out. She stood almost whispering her song, nervously rocking back and forth. I was down in the orchestra pit trying to cheer her on, but she was frozen with fright.

Then, she began staring at something, and little by little her voice grew stronger. I stopped even trying to direct and turned to see where she was looking. The student high up in the sound booth had his face against the window as he nodded and mouthed the words, "You can do it. You can do it." Suddenly, with a voice like Mahalia Jackson's, she belted, "We are the world," and she brought down the house. The "juvenile delinquent?" He shone like a bright new copper penny. And the boy with dyslexia? He didn't miss a word.

During those last few weeks of school, our chorus became an unstoppable force of nature with a television appearance, and invitations to sing at both Baccalaureate and Graduation.

The sad truth is, if I had known the past histories of the students I chose as leads, I would not have taken a risk with them. I'm glad all I knew to do was look for what the students did well.

But, may I tell you my favorite part of this story? Meri Beth and Molly knew the students, yet they never said one discouraging word to me about them. And afterwards, they rejoiced over the newly-realized potential of their fellow classmates---now turned superstars!

A Two-fold Promise
Life Lesson #38

*And my God will meet all your needs according to the riches
of his glory in Christ Jesus* (Philippians 4:19).

YOU CANNOT IMAGINE HOW MANY TIMES I HAVE
clung tightly to this promise. I love this verse and have found it to be true. Not
only does this scripture contain a promise, but also it is a two-fold promise.
God will meet all your needs. If the verse only said that, it would be wonderful
enough, but there is another component that makes it even more extraordinary.
He will meet your needs *according to the riches of his glory in Christ Jesus.* Wow!

And just how rich are *the riches of his glory in Christ Jesus*? Absolutely
as rich in every way as it's possible to be. God will meet our needs, and He
loves to surprise us with extras along the way, too!

I have learned a very valuable Life Lesson about God meeting our
needs. If we believe God's promises, we must realize that the answers may
not come until the 11th hour. That realization will relieve us of worry! Just
trust God, and wait.

Years ago, Wayne and I made a commitment to help some overseas missionaries with a very worthwhile ministry project. We needed a certain
amount of money so we could get it to them. We did not have it. So the
night before the money was needed, we put the checkbook on the dining
room table and laid our hands on it. We asked God to provide the money
so we could deposit it in time to keep our commitment to the missionaries.

The following day was nearing an end, and we still did not have the
money. We were not sure what we were going to do, but we agreed to
believe Philippians 4:19. That evening we went to a meeting of the Gideons
International. Wayne and I both appreciate their work in Bible distribution,
and we wanted to hear their reports on the Myrtle Beach Bible Blitz.

Before the meeting began, a young man handed me an envelope and
said his mother asked him to give it to us. I thanked him and put it in my
purse not knowing what the envelope contained. Several months previously
we had coordinated a community outreach ministry hosted by the young
man's mother.

The Gideons' meeting was very inspiring as we heard the reports and testimonies. After the meeting, I was almost out the door when a friend stopped me and gave me a small Gideon New Testament. As I thanked him and took it, he said, "Be careful, there's something in it."

That statement piqued my curiosity. When I got in the car, Wayne started to put the key in the ignition. I asked him to wait. "I've just been handed two items, and I'd like to see what they are."

I got the envelope from my purse and opened it. It was a check. Without us having any idea, the lady with whom we had done the community outreach event made a donation to our ministry. It was only $100.00 shy of the money we needed for the missionaries.

Then I opened the New Testament, and--you guessed it--a crisp $100.00 bill was inside. No one knew of the need, yet God used two different people to provide the exact amount needed for the missionaries. We experienced God fulfilling Philippians 4:19 at 9:30 that night! I sat in the car and cried as we praised God together for His faithfulness. We were able to deposit the money the next day and get it to the missionaries on time.

From the above experience and numerous others, I have learned:

- **God meets our needs.**
- **God meets them in greater ways than we can imagine.**
- **God's timing is always perfect. (After all, He sees the end from the beginning.)**
- **To avoid worry, trust God...and wait.**
- **When we become a child of the King, we inherit the riches of His glory in Christ Jesus!**

Whatever your need is today, please read and believe Philippians 4:19.

God's Voice
Life Lesson #39

...And God said...(Genesis 1:3a).

THE LIFE LESSONS THAT MEAN THE MOST TO ME ARE the ones through which I learn more about who God is. Some of these Life Lessons are so glorious they make me want to shout. Others are so holy they bring me to my knees.

This post is the first in a trio of Life Lessons I felt led to write as we reflect on God's voice. Today's lesson is a simple one on how the Bible describes God's voice. The next Life Lesson in entitled "When God Speaks," and the third Life Lesson in the trio will deal with "Hearing and Obeying God's Voice."

Each person's voice is completely unique. Just as no two fingerprints are the same, also no two voices are the same. Many corporations, and even governmental agencies, now use voice recognition as a means to secure identity.

Although a voice is composed of various elements, three of the main ones are phonation, pitch, and volume. Phonation (sound makers) are the result of air swishing through folds that run horizontally across the larynx, or voice box. Pitch is similar to frequency and is measured in Hertz (Hz). Volume, or loudness, is measured in decibels.

Can you imagine what God's voice is like? We will find out over the next few Life Lessons, but for now, we will look at scriptures that give us some insight into how His voice sounds. I'm excited about these lessons, and I hope they will be meaningful to you.

God's voice is powerful and full of majesty (Psalm 29:4).
God's voice is mighty (Psalm 68:33).
God's voice is like the sound of many waters (Ezekiel 43:2, Revelation 1:15, Jeremiah 10:13).
God's voice is like the sound of thunder (2 Samuel 22:14, Psalm 18:13).
God's voice is like the sound of angels' wings (Ezekiel 1:24, Ezekiel 10:5).
God's voice is like the sound of a trumpet (Revelation 1:10, Revelation 4:1).
God's voice is like a gentle blowing (still, small voice KJV) (I Kings 19:12).

God's voice comes from the throne (Revelation 19:5), out of heaven (Daniel 4:31, Matthew 3:17, Mark 1:11, Luke 3:22, John 12:28, 2 Peter 1:18), out of a cloud (Matthew 17:5, Mark 9:7, Luke 9:35), and from a burning bush (Acts 7:31).

Which description is most meaningful to you, and why?

When I taught deaf preschoolers at a local public school, most of the students who came to my class did not know words. In fact, most of them did not know there was such a thing as a word. Although teaching that concept was challenging, it also was rewarding when they realized everything they saw, touched, smelled, and tasted had a name that went with it, and that name was a word.

Once they understood words, I started increasing their vocabulary. I also taught them how to make the sounds of words. Among other things, I placed their little hands on the side of my neck to feel the vibrations certain sounds made. I put a feather in front of my lips to show them which sounds expelled air, as in words beginning with the letters *p* and *t*. I placed their hands on my lips to so they could feel the tickling vibration, "m-m-m," of the *m* sound.

I'll never forget the day one precious little girl excitedly waited for her mother after the other students left. I greeted her mother when she arrived and said, "Wendy has been working on a surprise for you." Her mother looked puzzled. I then turned to my student and did the sign for "Mother."

Wendy looked in her mother's eyes and slowly, but deliberately, said, "Ma-a-a-h, Ma-a-a-h." Her mother took Wendy in her arms and wept. It was the first time she had heard her five-year-old daughter refer to her as Mama. It was "a moment" for us all. A child's voice--though imperfect from her hearing loss--was probably the most beautiful sound that mother had ever heard.

Get ready. We are preparing to hear God's voice, and it well may be the most beautiful sound we will ever hear!

When God Speaks
Life Lesson #40

...Thus says the Lord...(Exodus 4:22 NKJV).

ACCORDING TO BIBLE.ORG, SOME FORM OF *GOD SAID* is used at least 3,800 times in scripture. So, God's voice is a very prominent theme of the Bible.

In the last Life Lesson, we saw God's voice is powerful and full of majesty; mighty; sounds like many waters, thunder, angels' wings, a trumpet; a gentle blowing (a still, small voice); and it has come from the throne, heaven, out of a cloud, and a burning bush.

One thing I've learned in my lifetime is when God speaks, things happen. They have to because He promised His Word will not return to Him empty but will accomplish what He intends (Isaiah 55:11).

Two schools of thought seem to prevail today. The first is God only spoke to people until His Word (the Bible) was completed. The other is God continues to speak to people today.

I am of the latter school of thought. I do believe God speaks to His children today through the Holy Spirit. However--and this is very important--when He speaks, He in one way or another acknowledges, confirms, clarifies, explains, teaches, applies, edifies, and/or guides through His holy Word.

God's Word is truth, and you simply can't improve on that! Nothing He could say would be any more wonderful than what He already has said. Jesus said, *'Sanctify them by the truth; your word is truth'* (John 17:17).

One reason I feel so strongly God continues to speak to us today is by observing His first institution--the human family. As I've stated before, God uses the natural to teach spiritual truths.

Marriage, birth, or adoption are the starting points for a relationship in the human family. However, the fellowship--or closeness--we experience with our family members depends on many factors, some of the most important being our communication and shared experiences. Could you imagine becoming a part of a family where the family unit never talks or interacts with each other?

In a real sense, marriage, birth, and adoption are also the starting points for a relationship in the spiritual family. At salvation we become the Bride of Christ (Revelation 19:7-9). Through the new birth we enter the family of God (John 1:12). We are adopted as children of God becoming joint-heirs with Christ Jesus (Romans 8:17).

It stands to reason if we are in a relationship with the Heavenly Father as part of His family, He wants to communicate with us. He desires for our fellowship--or closeness to Him--to increase. Therefore, He speaks to us, and when He does, things happen.

A warning: many well-meaning people say, "The Lord told me this," or "The Lord told me that," and all the while they unknowingly wrap their own personal opinions in holy language. Scripture tells us to be wise and discerning. If we allow God to do so, He will show us what is truly a word from Him versus what is someone's personal opinion. The Bible is the litmus test.

I remember when one of our church members said God told her Wayne should wear a tie to the Wednesday night prayer meetings. With all the starving people in the world, I didn't think Wayne dressing casually on Wednesday nights concerned God, so I checked that one off as a personal opinion. Sometimes you just have to smile!

When it's truly God speaking, great and mighty things happen. Let's look back through scripture and see a few of the things that happened when God spoke.

1. He called the world into existence (Genesis 1:1-31).
   God's voice speaks His truth, and truth is the foundation of the world!
2. He saved a righteous man and his family from destruction (Genesis 7:1-24).
3. He established a nation of people through whom He would reveal His plan of redemption (Genesis 17:5).
4. He gave His instructions for living (Exodus 20:1-17). (The "Ten Commandments" remain the basis for our judicial system.)
5. He established a kingdom that would not end (2 Samuel 7:16).
6. He warned of apostasy--the falling away from God. (Through various prophets)
7. He stopped a storm with the words, "Peace be still" (Mark 4:39).
8. He called forth a dead man buried in a tomb, and the man came alive (John 11:43).

9. He has promised He will come again (John 14:3). Are you ready for that day?

In conclusion, I think it is very important for us to realize God uses what He has spoken, particularly the accuracy of His prophecies, to prove He is the one true God (Isaiah 45:20-23; 46:9-10; 48:3-5).

I'm excited about the next Life Lesson, "Hearing and Obeying God's Voice." It was life-changing for me, and I pray it will be for you as well!

Hearing and Obeying God's Voice
Life Lesson #41

'My sheep listen to my voice...and they follow me' (John 10:27).

AS WE CONCLUDE OUR TRILOGY ABOUT "GOD'S Voice," I realize we have not covered everything. Such a glorious subject could provide a lifetime of lessons.

So, I thought perhaps a question and answer format might be helpful to conclude our series.

1. **How does God speak to us today?**

   God speaks through the Holy Spirit most often in a *still, small voice.* His voice conveys a thought or impression that comes to your heart, and you recognize it is not something you would have thought of on your own. Jesus said of the Holy Spirit: *'But the Advocate, the Holy Spirit, whom the Father will send in my name, will teach you all things and will remind you of everything'* (John 14:26).

2. **How can I know it's God's voice and not Satan (or some person) trying to confuse me?**

   God's voice always confirms His Word: *Dear friends, do not believe every spirit, but test the spirits to see whether they are from God, because many false prophets have gone out into the world* (I John 4:1). God promised He will give us discernment and wisdom if we ask Him (James 1:5).

3. **Is there anything that can prevent my hearing from God?**

   An unrepentant heart, unbelief, and disobedience will impede our ability to hear God's voice (Isaiah 59:2). However, I feel there are two other obstacles of which we might not even be aware.

a. We don't really expect to hear from God because we don't feel worthy of hearing from Him. Remember: God usually speaks directly to His child and confirms His Word through other people as He did with the young prophet Samuel in the Bible (I Samuel 7:3-10).

b. We don't know what to expect when He does speak. Most of us are waiting for God to "fuss at" us for what we have done, or are doing, wrong.

One day I realized a beautiful truth: God speaks to us in the same ways He teaches us to speak to each other.

The Bible says we are to...

Speak the truth in love (Ephesians 4:15).

Avoid quarreling, be gentle, show perfect courtesy (Titus 3:9).

Build up [edify] *as fits the occasion* (Ephesians 4:29).

Think [and since thoughts precede words---we are to speak] *whatever is true, honorable, just, pure, lovely, commendable, and worthy of praise* (Philippians 4:8).

Even when God chastises us, He does so with great love, showing us the truth of the matter (if we're open to truth) and building us up by reminding us how special we are to Him.

I'd like to end this lesson with two very important areas of "Hearing and Obeying God's Voice": **God's Love** and **God's Leadership**.

God's Love:

Sometimes we don't realize how much God loves us because we don't give Him a chance to tell us. We read of His love in scripture, but also He wants to confirm His love to us personally. I'd like to challenge you to take time to enjoy God's presence.

I find I do better if I simply spend time with God during my quiet time (usually over a cup of hot tea), and then at another time do Bible study and prayer requests. Reading a Psalm is a great way to come into His presence. Whatever works best for you, please try listening for God to tell you how special you are to Him.

Be prepared to be blessed! God loves you so much He will say things you would never say about yourself. Please let Him. He made you, and He takes great delight in you!

God's Leadership:

Wayne and I have found four things seem to converge when God is leading us into or away from an opportunity: the quickening (desire) of the heart; God's Word; timing; and circumstances. Peace is a powerful indicator of God's will!

By God's Word I don't mean "proof texting" (opening the Bible and pointing to a verse assuming it's the right scripture for the occasion). God rarely speaks through His Word in that way. However, if you have been reading, studying, meditating on His Word, and a passage stays with you, that is likely God at work.

Many years ago some of our good friends, Charles and Marlou, asked us to pray with them about a job offer in Little ***Rock***, Arkansas. The verse, "... *the wise man who built his house upon the **rock**...*" (Matthew 7:24) became their special scripture. However, the job closed and their house did not sell, but the verse remained in their hearts daily.

One year later, they called and excitedly told us they were moving to a dream job in Blowing ***Rock***, North Carolina! Quickening of the heart, God's Word, timing, and circumstances equal God's perfect peace.

'Speak, for Your servant is listening' (I Samuel 3:10).

Think Happy Thoughts
Life Lesson #42

I think myself happy...because I shall answer for myself this day (Acts 26:2 KJV).

WE HAVE JUST COMPLETED A SERIES OF LIFE LESSONS about God's voice, and thus His words. In the next lessons, we will look at the power and importance of *our* words. However, since our words come from our thoughts, we will first look at some Life Lessons about our thoughts.

We are as happy as we think we are. When Paul said, *'I think myself happy,'* he used a wonderful choice of words. We can either think ourselves happy, or think ourselves unhappy, because happiness is a state of mind.

Only we can control the thoughts we dwell on daily. Our thoughts evoke the emotions that lead to our behaviors, which eventually become our habits. Our habits, over a period of time, become our character.

King Solomon said, *'For as a man thinks in his heart, so is he'* (Proverbs 23:7 NKJV).

How can we *think ourselves happy* in the midst of troubling circumstances? One answer is found in Psalm 146:5: *Blessed is he whose help is in the God of Jacob, whose hope is in the Lord his God.*

What more could we need than the assurance of God's help, no matter what we are facing? That promise is our hope. That promise is our happiness. Dwelling on God's love and seeking His will keeps our thoughts where they should be--on Him.

I read a story about two construction workers who sat down to eat lunch. One opened his lunch box and began eating. The other pulled a sandwich out of his lunch bag and began complaining. He grumbled because he had another bologna sandwich. For five days straight he had eaten a bologna sandwich for lunch. Now here was another one! His co-worker suggested he tell his wife that he was tired of bologna. He looked at his friend and said, "My wife? I fix my own lunches."

We are the ones who put the "bologna" in our minds. We, like Paul, can change our thought patterns by *thinking ourselves happy.*

In our next Life Lesson, we will delve into this subject more thoroughly as we look at transforming our minds (Romans 12:2). However, I'd like to set the stage by presenting the fact that we *do* have the power to change our mindsets. As our scriptures show, God wants to be our *help* and our *hope* in this endeavor.

In closing, please consider these two questions:

1. If your happy thoughts were graded on a score with 100% being perfect, what percentage of your thoughts would be happy thoughts?
2. When you recognize unhappy thoughts dominating, make a "jot list" of the good things that have happened to you throughout the day to overcome the negative thoughts.

Many years ago, our daughter, Molly, was helping teach first graders in our church's Vacation Bible School. One of the students became nauseated in the hallway. When Molly saw the expressions on the faces of the children, she was afraid a chain reaction might happen, so she encouraged the children to pray for everyone to be well and not to dwell on what they had just seen, but to think only of happy things.

As the children walked down the hall, one of the first graders, Courtney, and Molly smiled at each other and began repeating, "Think happy thoughts! Think happy thoughts!"

Five years later, we were moving from Myrtle Beach for Wayne to pastor in Boone, North Carolina. Our church in Myrtle Beach planned a beautiful farewell banquet. Afterwards, as people were leaving, Courtney hugged us and with tears streaming down her face she said, "Think happy thoughts! Think happy thoughts!"

Hearing her sweet little child's voice say those words caused me to break down in tears. Still, it is true, reminding ourselves to think happy thoughts can help us face some of the toughest circumstances in life.

Please take time this week to list things that make you happy. Dwell on these things, and you just might "think yourself happy."

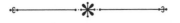

TRANSFORMING OUR MINDS
LIFE LESSON #43

HAVE YOU EVER WISHED FOR A "DO OVER?" I ENJOY watching movies like "Miss Congeniality" in which a character has a complete transformation. The Bible tells us sometimes we need do overs. Consider the following verse: *Do not conform to the pattern of this world, but be transformed by the renewing of your mind. Then you will be able to test and approve what God's will is – his good, pleasing and perfect will* (Romans 12:2).

As I mentioned in the last Life Lesson, we will begin a study on the importance of our words. But since our words are preceded by our thoughts, we will first consider the importance of our thoughts.

The above scripture from Romans 12:2 is very powerful. It not only gives us the way to transform our lives, but also it gives us the way to salvation.

The verse begins with a warning: *Do not conform to the pattern of this world*. I don't think I've ever seen a time in my life when people conform to the pattern of this world any more than they do today. Have you? Rather than, "Is it right?" today's question has become "Is it popular?"

The Bible tells us not to conform to the pattern of the world, so how do we break that pattern? The verse further explains we can be *transformed* by the *renewing* of our minds.

Renewing our minds is an awesome opportunity as well as a scriptural mandate. The Greek word used in this verse for *renew* comes from the Greek word which means "completing a process." It also can mean "make fresh, new, see properly, a new development, a renewal achieved by God's power."

The previous Life Lesson dealt with thinking happy thoughts or changing from troubling thoughts to happy thoughts. A couple of years ago, several things were happening that were "downers." Wayne woke up late one night and came into the dining room and found me at the table playing Pharrell Williams's song, "Happy," on the computer. As I jammed with the music, he asked me what I was doing. I smiled and said, "I needed this." He smiled and went back to bed. What are some of the things you do to renew your mind to *think happy thoughts*?

I especially like one of the definitions for the Greek word, *renew*--"seeing properly." I believe personalizing the prayer Elisha prayed for his servant in

2 Kings 6:17a, truly does open our eyes to truths we would not normally recognize. This tiny prayer is powerful: '*Open his* [my] *eyes, Lord, and let him* [me] *see.*' On the days I make it a point to pray this prayer, I am much more aware of God working in my life and in the lives of others. In other words, I am "seeing properly." Will you agree to pray this prayer often, and journal some of the things that happen in your life as a result?

Philippians 4:8 provides us with the perfect filter through which to sift all our thoughts: *Finally, brothers and sisters, whatever is true, whatever is noble, whatever is right, whatever is pure, whatever is lovely, whatever is admirable – if anything is excellent or praiseworthy – think about such things.* True, noble, right, pure, lovely, admirable, excellent or praiseworthy comprise a list of beautiful attributes. In considering this list, how many of your daily thoughts pass this test? If you did not pass the test, will you plan to do something about it, with God's help?

Finally, the more we focus on Jesus, the more the Holy Spirit will help us renew our minds. Isn't that amazing? The more we think about Jesus, the more like Him we become. *In your relationships with one another, have the same mindset* ["mind" KJV] *as Christ Jesus* (Philippians 2:5). Now that's transformation!

True transformation comes from the inside out. As our minds are renewed, our whole being is transformed. I think it's no coincidence Romans 12:1 talks about *presenting your body as a living sacrifice* right before we're told to be transformed by the renewing of our minds. Renewing the mind affects the whole body!

I mentioned the movie "Miss Congeniality" in the beginning. It's about an awkward and shabbily-dressed detective assigned as an undercover agent posing as a contestant in a beauty pageant. A team of hired experts made her beautiful on the outside. However, she wasn't transformed until she began to think of herself as a real beauty contestant.

What is the result of renewing our minds? Not only will we be happier; not only will we "see properly" and not have out-of-focus thoughts; not only will our thoughts be sifted through the attributes of Philippians 4:8; not only will we grow in Christlikeness, but also we will be able to discern God's will--*His good, pleasing and perfect will!* A powerful verse revealing a vital message, Romans 12:2.

The "Heart" of the Matter
Life Lesson #44

IN TODAY'S LIFE LESSON, I'D LIKE TO GO ONE STEP deeper and look at how our hearts influence our thoughts before moving on to the power of our words. The following verses say it well:

As he thinks in his heart, so is he (Proverbs 23:7 NKJV).

For the mouth speaks what the heart is full of (Luke 6:45).

The Bible places a clear responsibility on us to control our thoughts: *Take every thought captive so that it conforms to the will of God* (2 Corinthians 10:5). In addition, the Bible also says our thoughts come out of our hearts: *For it is from within, out of a person's heart, that evil thoughts come--sexual immorality, theft, murder, adultery, greed, malice, deceit, lewdness, envy, slander, arrogance and folly. All these evils come from inside and defile a person* (Mark 7:21-23).

Let me preface this Life Lesson by saying a biblical study of the heart is deep and rich, but we only have space to touch on it here.

In school, I was taught that the brain signals the heart to beat. Yet modern research shows the heartbeat of a fetus in the womb begins long before the brain is even formed. I think that's remarkable!

So then, exactly what is "the heart?" The Hebrew word, *lebab*, and the Greek word, *kardia*, can refer to the actual human heart organ. However, their definitions, and various scriptures, show the heart is far more complex than a beating muscle. It represents the innermost part of the human. It is...

- the center of one's being (Proverbs 4:23).
- the true nature of a person's character (I Samuel 16:7; Luke 6:45).
- associated with the mind, will, and emotions (Psalm 4:7; Isaiah 65:14; Proverbs 12:25).
- the seat of the conscience (Job 27:6; Romans 2:15).
- the place where a person believes and exercises his or her faith and communes with God (Luke 24:25, Romans 10:9,10).

Harris's theological Wordbook of the Old Testament says in its abstract form the heart is "the richest biblical term for the totality of man's inner or immaterial nature." In other words, the heart is who we are at the very core, and it affects our thinking. Our hearts can either defile us (Matthew 12:34), or purify us (Psalm 24:4).

Jesus always emphasized the importance of the condition of a person's heart.

The pure in heart see God (Matthew 5:8).

Sin is first committed in the heart (Matthew 5:28).

Evil thoughts and acts come from the heart (Matthew 15:19).

Forgiveness comes from the heart (Matthew 18:35).

We must love God with all our heart (Matthew 22:37).

God's Word is sown and responded to in the heart (Luke 8:11-15).

So, if both evil thoughts and good thoughts come from the heart, and we're told to take control of our thoughts, how can we do that?

The heart is deceitful above all things, and desperately wicked; who can know [understand] *it* (Jeremiah 17:9 NKJV)? Unfortunately we, like Eve, choose disobedience from the get-go, and our hearts are defiled.

The following words are crucial words: Only God can change our hearts. Our part is to be willing to let Him. The more we reject Him, the harder our hearts become. The more open we are to His truths, the more open to Him our hearts become.

God's gift of grace offered through the sacrificial death of Jesus is the only way our hearts can be changed. When we accept that gift, our hearts are made new. The indwelling of the Holy Spirit takes place at that moment giving us the power to *think happy thoughts*, and choose to dwell on things that are true, noble, etc. (Philippians 4:8).

I sometimes tell children our hearts become dirty and yucky when we do things we know are wrong. I ask them to try to clean out their hearts. Of course, they can't. So I explain when they accept the gift Jesus offers them through His death on the cross, even though they can't see it happen, He cleans out their hearts and makes them fresh and bright.

Once our hearts are regenerated through salvation, the work is completed--forever! However, the Bible shows us how to best maintain our spiritual heart-health: *Above all else, guard your heart, for everything you do flows from it* (Proverbs 4:23).

Proverbs 4:24-26 shows us how to guard our hearts: *Keep your mouth free of perversity; keep corrupt talk far from your lips. Let your eyes look straight ahead; fix your gaze directly before you. Give careful thought to the paths of your feet and be steadfast in all your ways. Do not turn to the right or the left; keep your foot from evil.*

In other words, we must guard our hearts by watching what we say, do, and the choices we make. Have you allowed God to change your heart? Today could be your day of salvation.

The Power of Words
Life Lesson #45

The tongue has the power of life and death, and those that love it [to talk] *will eat its fruit* (Proverbs 18:21).

YOU'VE SEEN IT, AND I HAVE TOO. ONE WORD changes the entire atmosphere in a room, for better or for worse. How can only one word carry such power? The preceding Life Lessons showed our words come from our thoughts, and our thoughts come from our hearts. Since the heart is the seat of our emotions, it makes sense our words often convey our feelings.

Amazingly, most of the *words* we use to communicate are not even spoken. It's true. Although the exact numbers in his findings have been disputed, Professor Dr. Albert Mehrabian conducted various studies concluding communication is 55% body language, 38% tone of voice, and only 7% the actual words spoken. If you are in a group and only one person is speaking, you sense what the others are thinking by observing their body language. Crossed arms, looking the other way, sighs, etc., scream boredom--even rudeness. Paying attention, smiling, nodding, clapping, etc., indicate affirmation and interest. So, as we consider the impact of our spoken words, please also take into consideration our nonverbal communication. Ralph Waldo Emerson is attributed by some with saying, "What you do speaks so loudly, I can't hear what you say."

When I started writing this Life Lesson, I once again realized it cannot be covered in one lesson, so we will continue it through a few more lessons. I'm praying for clarity in how to present these truths, because I know the impact words have had on my life both positively and negatively. I remember positive words spoken to me, and I smile, or feel a sense of peace. I remember hurtful words spoken to me, and I feel a knot form in my stomach. "Sticks and stones will break my bones, but words will never harm me" is *not* true.

In the ministry, we deal with many different situations. I want to say to anyone reading this who has lived in a verbally abusive situation, I pray somehow you can find a healing peace through these lessons. God bless you!

The Bible has much to say about the importance of words. In our opening verse, we read words contain the power of life and death. I hope by the end of this series, you will see how that is possible.

Before going further, let's consider a few interesting things about words.

Uniqueness of our words:

Did you know we humans are the only species that use words? (Parrots can only copy words.) So far, researchers have not found a single people group in the world who does not use words. God gave us the ability to communicate with Him in the way He communicates with us---through words. After all, *In the beginning was the Word, and the Word was with God, and the Word was God* (John 1:1).

Longevity of our words:

Words are energy, and according to scientists, energy can't be destroyed; it merely changes form. So, I guess you could say our words never die. When you think of it in that way, it makes you want to watch carefully what you say, doesn't it?

Influence of our words:

Scripture tells us God spoke the world into existence. Have you ever thought about how we, in a sense, speak our worlds (events around us) into existence? When we constantly complain, or speak negatively about how bad our lives and the people in them are, we believe what we say, and we come to expect the worst instead of God's best. The opposite is also true. Researchers say 90% of what we say about ourselves is negative. I don't remember reading any passage in the Bible where Jesus put himself down, do you?

Purpose of our words:

In the next lesson we will look at some very specific ways we are to use, and not use, our words. As we prepare for those lessons, please consider the following verses:

My tongue shall talk of your righteousness and of your praise all the day long (Psalm 35:28).

Let no corrupting thought come out of your mouth, but only such as is good for building up, as fits the occasion, that I may give grace to those who hear (Ephesians 4:32).

What loftier purpose could there be than praising God and building up other people? Is that how we choose to use our words?

We only travel the journey of life once. May we choose wisely the powerful words we speak, and the way we speak them! Enjoy the journey!

Wonderful Words of Life
Life Lesson #46

When I was a child, I learned the song, "Wonderful Words of Life." The opening stanza began, "Sing them over again to me, wonderful words of life. Let me more of their beauty see, wonderful words of life."

In the next lesson in our series on words, we will look at what the Bible says about our hurtful words, and the following lesson, "Taming My Tongue." However, today we'll consider Biblical instructions on how to use our "Wonderful Words of Life."

SPEAKING WORDS OF LIFE:

1. **Praising God is the most beautiful use of language.**
   I will extol the Lord at all times; his praise will always be on my lips (Psalm 34:1). Do you include a vast vocabulary of wonderful, beautiful words to praise and adore God? He's so wonderful, let's make that practice a daily habit.

2. **Witnessing is the best way to put our praise into action.**
   And whatever you do, whether in word or deed, do it all in the name of the Lord Jesus, giving thanks to God the Father through him (Colossians 3:17).

3. **Think before we speak.**
   Let everyone be quick to listen, slow to speak, slow to anger (James 1:19). We can't take back our words after we speak them. Once we utter a word, it will either help or hurt someone. Rarely is it neutral. As the old saying goes, each of us should "put our mind into gear before we put our mouth into motion." I've never heard anyone regret saying kind words to another person, but the opposite is true with unthoughtful words spoken in haste or retaliation.

4. Our words should build up (edify) and encourage others.
Let your conversation be always with grace seasoned with salt, that you may know how you ought to answer everyone (Colossians 4:6). I love this verse! As challenging as it is, speaking with grace seasoned with salt is what we're instructed to do.

What does the phrase, *always with grace,* mean? In the secular sense, *grace* means, "simple elegance, courteous goodwill, an attractively polite manner of behaving." In the spiritual sense, it means "unmerited favor from God."

The Greek word for "grace," *charis,* is in the same family group as the word "forgive." Do you see the significance? Grace and forgiveness go hand in hand and affect our words.

Seasoned with salt is an interesting description. Biblically, salt added flavor, was used to preserve foods, and even was used as a medicine. Thus, our words should add flavor when we speak, and they should preserve peace, and promote healing. Can you imagine how different the world would be if we tried to live by this one verse alone?

Do not let any unwholesome talk come out of your mouths, but only what is helpful for building others up according to their needs, that it may benefit those who listen (Ephesians 4:29). Our words should be so uplifting they even benefit those who overhear them.

Wayne flew to Texas several years ago. During a conversation with the man beside him, he learned the man was going to Texas for his grandson's funeral. Wayne tried to minister to him, and he prayed with him.

In the aisle as the passengers exited the plane a young man, who had been seated on the row in front of Wayne, turned and said he could not help but overhear Wayne's conversation with the bereaved man. He said it meant a lot to him because, even though he was a youth minister himself, he wasn't sure what he would have said to the grieving grandfather. As they walked into the airport, Wayne thanked him. Then several other people joined the young man. Wayne looked from one to the other and said, "I know you. You're 'Casting Crowns!'" He then prayed with the group for their concert that night in the Dallas Cowboys' Stadium.

Wayne's edification of the sorrowful grandfather benefited a member of a very popular contemporary Christian singing group who happened to overhear the conversation. Do we benefit those who hear our conversations?

5. **Learn to speak the truth in love.**
    Therefore, each of you must put off falsehood and speak truthfully to your neighbor, for we are all members of one body (Ephesians 4:25). God expects us to use our words to maintain unity rather than cause division (Ephesians 4:3).

We can be truthful, yet kind. Ephesians 4:15 tells us: "*...speaking the truth in love, we will grow to become in every respect the mature body of him who is the head, that is, Christ.*" Some people and issues need to be confronted, but it is a sign of maturity in Christ when we are honest while *speaking the truth in love*.

If we put the above scriptures into action, we will be blessed...and we will be a blessing! I could write much more, but let's close this Life Lesson by prayerfully reading the following passage:

...be filled with the Spirit speaking to one another with psalms, hymns, and songs from the Spirit. Sing and make music in your heart to the Lord (Ephesians 5:18b-19).

You can do it!

You Don't Say
Life Lesson #47

Reckless words pierce like a sword, but the tongue of the wise brings healing (Proverbs 12:18).

THE EXPRESSION "YOU DON'T SAY" OFTEN IS USED when someone hears interesting news or information. Some time ago, a popular word game show aired with the title, "You Don't Say!" Based on the show, we started playing our own family version of the game. The grandchildren love it, and Wayne and I still play it in the car when we're traveling.

The truth is, what you *don't* say is as important as what you *do* say--sometimes even more so. It's usually more difficult to refrain from saying what you should not say than it is to say what you should.

The Bible is clear about hurtful words. I'd like to list a few things the Bible says *you don't say*. I pray this is helpful is some way.

The Bible says: *Death and life are in the power of the tongue* (Proverbs 18:21). Have you ever thought about just how powerful our words can be? They affect us and the ones to whom we are speaking.

Words of Life or Death:

The Hebrew word for *death* in the verse above concretely means "the dead, their place or state," and figuratively, it means "pestilence and ruin." Our words do have the power to ruin another person's life. We need to always keep that truth in mind.

Words used in the wrong way are equated *with bitterness, wrath, anger, clamor, evil speaking, malice, sexual impurity, uncleanness (impurity), coveting, and idolatry* (Matthew 15:19; Colossians 3:8; Ephesians 4:21, 29-30; Ephesians 5:3-5; and Matthew 7:17). *Those things that proceed out of the mouth come from the heart* (Matthew 15:18). Our words are really a reflection of our hearts.

You can tell a person's character by their words and by the way they respond to insults and put-downs spoken to them. In the previous Life Lesson, we discussed *speaking the truth in love* which is a positive indicator of a good character (*clean heart* in Psalm 51:10). It's certainly a goal for us all.

Destroying Unity:

The Bible instructs us: *Make every effort to keep the unity of the Spirit through the bond of peace* (Ephesians 4:3). I believe our words are the most effective way to fulfill this command, because our words can either build or destroy unity and the bond of peace. As goes the tongue, so goes the church, or any relationship. Even though Paul was addressing a church in this verse, this principle is true in every relationship.

The following are some of the ways our words destroy unity in relationships:

1. **Lying**
   A lie is a tool of Satan. In fact, Jesus said of Satan '*...there is no truth in him. When he lies, he speaks his native language, for he is a liar and the father of lies*' (John 8:44).

   We speak Satan's language when we lie. He tries to destroy unity and alienate people from God and each other. Most of the time, he uses lies to accomplish his purposes. Don't fall for his schemes! He uses the same tactic over and over--lies and misperception of truth.

2. **Gossip**
   Gossip is not only hurtful, it is sinful. We all like to be in the know, and that position makes us more open to blatant gossiping: *A perverse person stirs up conflict, and a gossip separates close friends* (Proverbs 16:28). Gossip is an absolute unity buster.

3. **Evil speaking**

    Paul often addressed Christian conduct--especially concerning our words: *Nor should there be obscenity, foolish talk or coarse joking, which are out of place, but rather thanksgiving* (Ephesians 5:4). Do your words fall into the categories on this list?
    Obscenity (cursing)
    Foolish talk or coarse joking (abusiveness)
    Joking (inappropriate sarcasm)

4. **Complaining**

    When we complain, we speak against thankfulness and against trust in God. God takes complaining seriously. The punishment of the wilderness wanderings is an example of how serious complaining really is: *Do everything without grumbling or arguing* (Philippians 2:14). *For without faith it is impossible to please God...* (Hebrews 11:6a).

Again, there's so much more that could be included in this Life Lesson, but I'd like to close with some things that help me. I'm trying to grow in the area of controlling my words. I've found a verse that really helps me. I often pray it in situations where I might be tempted to say more than I should: *Set a guard over my mouth, Lord; keep watch over the door of my lips* (Psalm 141:3).

Finally, I'd like you to learn to quote this scripture as a protection when people speak negative, hurtful, or evil words into your life:

'No weapon forged against you [me] *will prevail, and you* [I] *will refute every tongue that accuses you* [me]. *This is the heritage of the servants of the Lord, and this is their vindication from me,' declares the Lord* (Isaiah 54:17).

Taming My Tongue
Life Lessons #48

For whoever would love life and see good days must keep their tongue from evil and their lips from deceitful speech (I Peter 3:10).

A LADY WENT TO A DOCTOR WITH A SORE TONGUE. When she told him her ailment he said, "Get some rest." She was angry and said he had not even looked at her tongue. He answered, "No, but I know it needs some rest."

I think it is true with most of us - our tongues could use some rest. For the past few lessons we've looked at our words including things we should and should not say. Today we end with the nuts and bolts of how to put what we've discussed into action.

Please read James 3:5-12 for a profound treatise on how the tongue can either be destructive or useful. Even though it is such a small part of the body, the tongue has great power. Taming it is one of the most useful skills we can develop in life.

Again, the Bible is clear on this issue. I've selected various scriptures to conclude our series. Learning to tame my tongue can make the difference between a life of peace or turmoil. Since I've titled this Life Lesson "Taming *My* Tongue," I will address the points in first person rather than third person. I'm still a work in progress with all the Life Lessons.

Heart Check:
What comes out of my mouth reflects what's in my heart. I do not have the power in my own strength to tame my tongue. I can only accomplish this when I allow God to cleanse my heart and purify my tongue.

Even though the following prayer is a small one, it is packed with power: *Let the words of my mouth and the meditation of my heart be acceptable in Your sight, O Lord, my strength and my Redeemer* (Psalm 19:14 NKJV). Praying this short prayer helps me stay focused on both my heart and my tongue.

Rely on the Holy Spirit:
Jesus promised the Holy Spirit will guide me in what to say (and not to say.) Most of the time when I speak out of turn, I've had a nudging from the Holy Spirit not to say something, but because I felt justified in saying it, I ignored the warning. Then I regretted it. Jesus said, *'For the Holy Spirit will teach you at that time what you should say'* (Luke 12:12).

Think before speaking:
Let everyone be quick to listen, slow to speak, and slow to anger (James 1:19). Have you ever found yourself pretending to listen to someone who was speaking, but you actually were busy mentally plotting what you were going to say next?

I'm still trying to grow in the area of reflective listening instead of speaking over another person. At some point in my life, I realized what others have to say is valuable, and I should clear my thoughts enough to listen to what they say. (Well, with really verbose people I guess I still just half-listen.)

Pray before speaking:
As I mentioned in the previous Life Lesson, I often pray, *'Set a guard over my mouth, Lord; keep watch over the door of my lips'* (Psalm 141:3). This verse is especially helpful when I know I will be in a potentially volatile situation.
One day a friend, Sylvia, called before a very anti-God woman was coming into her beauty shop, and she asked me to help her pray the woman's words would not affect the other customers. We prayed together over the phone using the above verse as a prayer. Later my friend called and said the most amazing thing happened. The woman would start to say something, and she'd stop and look puzzled stating she couldn't remember what she was going to say. Sylvia said at one time, it seemed as if the words literally could not come out of her mouth, so she just stopped trying to talk. Psalm 141:3 is a powerful prayer, indeed!

Remember, these could be your last words to someone:
Many of you have shared with me how you've been blessed by something our younger daughter, Molly, said to you or by a note she wrote to you. Her words are carefully chosen like a beautiful tapestry weaving a picture of heartfelt love.

When Molly was a little girl, she was very shy and had a hard time verbalizing her emotions. I remember how I worked with her trying to help her see the importance of being able to express her feelings. She started by leaving us little love notes in different places. Then she began speaking her feelings.

Recently I asked Molly how she so easily can show and speak love to others. She thanked me and reminded me she learned early in life that you never know when the words you are speaking to someone will be the last time you'll have a chance to make him or her feel valued as a person and loved by God. (Her paternal grandparents died when she and her sister, Meri Beth, were very young.)

Just realizing that truth should be enough to help me with the ongoing discipline of taming *my* tongue.

On the Other Side of Terrible
Life Lesson #49

The righteous cry out, and the Lord hears them; he delivers them from all their troubles. The Lord is close to the broken-hearted and saves those who are crushed in spirit (Psalm 34:17-18).

ARE YOU, OR SOMEONE CLOSE TO YOU, IN THE MIDST of a *terrible* time? Our family was recently. Some months ago, we were looking forward to our fourth grandchild, but the precious little one did not make it into our arms. Meri Beth and Thomas allowed Ty to choose the name of his sibling in heaven, and he named the baby, Avery. Then, a few weeks later our precious granddaughter, Mazi Grace, became extremely sick, and the doctors had a difficult time with the diagnosis. She was in the Children's Hospital of the Medical University of South Carolina in Charleston for eleven days followed by a long recovery.

So, in the midst of *terrible* times, how do we get to the other side? Frankly, when I wrote this Life Lesson, I was still on this journey, but I realized there were certain things I had to recognize in order to end up "On the Other Side of Terrible." I pray this personal Life Lesson will help you in some way. If you're in a *terrible* time, please consider this little acrostic, and the principles therein, to help move from where you are to where God wants you to be:

T - Truth

With tough times, misperceptions abound. As the saying goes, "When emotion runs high, logic runs low." We think in extremes rather than rationalities.

We also tend to look at the circumstances through the lens of how they make us feel. Then we begin to believe what we feel is reality. Satan is alive and well, and he always uses a lie (distortion of the truth) as his fiercest weapon.

Please seek the truth of the matter. God loves truth, and He will help us discern the truth and break our chains of misconceptions: *Then you will know the truth, and the truth will set you free* (John 8:32).

E - Eternity
Even during the worst of times, keeping an eternal perspective on life makes the challenges more bearable. In Christ we have the hope of eternal life free of the *terrible* things we experience in this fallen world. Heaven will be wonderful--life filled with love, joy, peace and free from sin, sickness, sorrow, and death: *For our light and momentary troubles are achieving for us an eternal glory that far outweighs them all* (2 Corinthians 4:17).

R - Reach out
Sometimes we can find answers or come to peace on our own, but at other times, we need to reach out for help. Some possible resources are people who have been through similar experiences, clergy, counselors and/or various support groups. Help is available, so please reach out for help when necessary: *Carry each other's burdens, and in this way you will fulfill the law of Christ* (Galatians 6:2).

R - Remember
One of the best ways to increase our faith is to remember how God brought us through *terrible* times in the past. David referred to this often in the Psalms: *I will remember the deeds of the LORD; yes, I will remember your miracles of long ago* (Psalm 77:11). Look back at God's goodness in order to look forward to His blessings! Trusting in the proven character of God rather than in the ways we think He should act increases our faith.

I - Investigate your options
Whether our *terrible* is physical, financial, relational, emotional, or anything else, options are available to help us. It's a matter of desiring to move forward and then exploring ways to do so. Sometimes it's trial and error. Sometimes it's giant steps. Sometimes it's little baby steps. But God wants to see us through, and He will help us build an action plan: *'For I know the plans I have for you' declares the Lord, 'plans for welfare and not for evil, to give you a future and a hope'* (Jeremiah 29:11 ESV).

B - Believe
Believe the promises of God. The Bible is full of the most beautiful promises we could ever want or need for any situation we face in life. One of the most beautiful of all is God is with us even through the *terrible*: *For no matter how*

many promises God has made, they are 'Yes' in Christ. And so through him the 'Amen' is spoken by us to the glory of God (2 Corinthians 1:20).

L - Learn

What can we learn from this experience that will help us become a stronger person or enable us to help others? Lessons abound in all of life and the Master Teacher longs to educate us if we're open: *'Take my yoke upon you and learn from me'* (Matthew 11:29).

E - Embrace the experience

When we are in the midst of *terrible*, we tend to become so consumed by the circumstances, we fail to see the blessings around us. Embracing all of life helps us put heartache in perspective. I heard Michael J. Fox say in an interview that sometimes he tries to embrace his Parkinson's by realizing, "This is what is happening to me at this moment. For now, I'll just go with it." What a powerful statement!

Paul expressed it this way, *'...for I have learned to be content whatever the circumstances'* (Philippians 4:11).

You may have noticed that each time I wrote the word, *terrible*, I wrote it in italics. Often our greatest blessings emerge from our deepest heart-aches, and what appears to be *terrible* is somehow and in some way actually not so *terrible* after all. If we look hard enough, our blessings far outweigh the *terrible*.

And remember, the words "terrible" and "terrific" both come from the same Latin verb. I pray for each hurting heart out there to find the terrific waiting for you "On the Other Side of Terrible!"

Doubly Clean
Life Lesson #50

...He saved us through the washing of rebirth and renewal by the Holy Spirit... (Titus 3:5).

PEGGY WAS HIRED AS A PERSONAL TEACHER'S AIDE for a student with severe developmental delays and partial deafness, and they both became part of my preschool classroom for the deaf. She was a wonderful aide and was full of hilarious witticisms. I enjoyed working with her. (The character of "Tilda," in my up-coming novel, is somewhat based on her.)

If she especially liked something, she would cross her arms over her large chest and say "um-hum," and for some reason that would make me laugh. During class, I often sat on the floor to teach the children. One day, as she watched me work with the students, Peggy admitted previously when she saw me walk down the hall with the small number of students in my class she would say, "That woman's got it made!" She went on to say, "But now that I'm in here and see all you do...well, all I can say is 'A heap sees, but only a few knows.'" Don't you love that statement? A lot of people see and judge a person accordingly, but only a few actually know what the person is going through.

However, one of my personal favorites was when I tried very hard to get across a concept to the students that was foundational for future learning. After a while, Peggy said, "Brown, don't you know what don't come out in da wash will come out in da rinse?" Once again, she made me laugh.

Recently, a mother shared with me her concern over her son's laundry while he is away in college. She felt sure he would not spot clean before putting things in the washer. "Oh, well," she said, "at least he'll have two chances to get it clean--the wash and the rinse."

I immediately thought of Peggy's phrase years ago. It is true the wash cycle gets out the stains, dirt, grime, and grease (or at least we hope it does.) Then the rinse cycle removes the detergent and any other residue left in the fabric (or at least we hope it does.)

While talking with that mother, like a lightning bolt, I realized God also gives us two chances to become clean. The first is the once-and-forever cleansing. When we, in faith, allow God to do His work in our lives, the stains, dirt, grime, and grease of our lives, and the sinful condition of our hearts, are cleansed by the blood of Jesus Christ: *For in Him we have redemption through his blood, the forgiveness of sins, in accordance with the riches of God's grace* (Ephesians 1:7).

Then, through God's Word, we have daily cleansing to help us overcome the trials and temptations of life: *...Christ loved the church and gave himself for her to make her holy, cleansing her by the washing of water through the word* (Ephesians 5:25, 26). The more immersed in God's Word we are, the easier it is to stay clean. I guess "cleanliness really is next to godliness" after all!

We see the pattern throughout scripture---first, the eternal cleansing from our sinful condition when we accept the atoning work of Jesus Christ, and then the perpetual cleansing from the works of the flesh through God's Word.

When the centurion speared Jesus' side on the cross, blood and water flowed from the wound (John 19:34). I find that sequence amazing!

I appreciate all the work our washing machines do. Wayne and I laughingly say we don't know how two people can accumulate so much laundry. But with all of us, our washing machines do a lot to get our clothes clean. As I mention a few things they do, please think of how this relates to you spiritually.

1. One of the main parts of the washing machine is the agitator.
    Sin agitates our minds and hearts, and that agitation can lead to seeking God: *Anxiety in a man's heart weighs it down...* (Proverbs 12:25).
2. The rinse cycle actually rinses the clothes more than once.
    We are cleansed by the blood of Jesus, and we receive a cleansing renewal through God's Word: *...washing of rebirth and renewal by the Holy Spirit* (Titus 3:5).

3. During the spin cycle, the washing machine swirls the clothes around in a circle.

Often we run around in circles trying to figure out life on our own, but God is in control. He longs to make us clean and keep us clean: *whiter than snow* (Psalm 51:7); *without spot or wrinkle or any other blemish* (Ephesians 5:27).

Have you allowed Him to wash and rinse you clean? Then, and only then, can you be "Doubly Clean!"

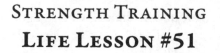

Strength Training
Life Lesson #51

I REMEMBER THE FIRST TIME I TRIED STRENGTH training. At the time, I did cardiovascular exercises regularly, but I decided it was time to start using weights. I went to the gym even though I didn't have a trainer. I watched how other people used the weights, so I copied them. I honestly did not know you were supposed to begin with light weights, do minimal repetitions, and perform only a few sets. So, in my zest to take my physical fitness up a notch, I did multiple reps and sets with heavier weights than I should have used.

The next day I walked around like someone in a body cast. The only muscles that did not hurt were the ones in my face. (I'm just glad I didn't do any physical harm to my body.) Believe me, I learned my lesson well.

Tucked away in a Bible verse is God's formula for spiritual strength training which is both infallible and eternal:

...the joy of the Lord is your strength (Nehemiah 8:10).

The history of this little verse is quite interesting. After a civil war, Israel divided into two kingdoms--Israel in the north and Judah in the south. Through various prophets, God warned those who refused to repent they would be taken from their homeland as captives into foreign countries. Eventually, Israel was exiled into Assyria and Judah into Babylon.

Today's verse speaks of Judah. Following seventy years of displacement in Babylon, the Jewish captives who desired to return to their homeland were allowed to leave in order to rebuild the temple in Jerusalem.

After the temple and the city walls were rebuilt, a scribe named Ezra held a public reading of God's law, and Nehemiah and the Levites helped explain its meaning. The people were so moved by what they heard, they became remorseful for not having kept God's Word, and they began to weep. They cried deep, wretched sobs of sorrow. The leaders instructed them not to cry but to rejoice. *The joy of the Lord* would be their strength.

The joy of the Lord--what a wonderful blessing God makes available to us! The Word of God quickens our hearts to mournful repentance, but it also gladdens our hearts by revealing God's mercy and forgiveness. *The joy of the Lord* is founded on a reconciled relationship with God!

Satan tries with all his might to rob us of our joy. He comes to *steal, kill, and destroy* (John 10:10). What is he trying to *steal, kill, and destroy*? Our joy, for he knows therein is our spiritual strength.

One tactic Satan uses repeatedly is to cause us to become so focused on our past mistakes and our wretchedness as sinners we miss the joy that comes with regeneration: *Godly sorrow brings repentance that leads to salvation and leaves no regret...*(2 Corinthians 7:20). Once we truly repent, the godly sorrow that led to our repentance leaves no regrets--only joy!

Don't allow Satan to keep you wailing and wallowing in the mire of past sins. Rather, accept the joy that comes with repentance and God's forgiveness. Most of us regret the past or fear the future, and we miss the joy of the present!

The people of Judah taught us a valuable lesson in Nehemiah 8:1-18. They reaffirmed their covenant with God and denounced their sins, observing the Feast of Tabernacles for the first time in many decades. We are told in Nehemiah 12:43 *the sound of rejoicing in Jerusalem could be heard far away*. They had regained their joy--and thus their strength!

How strong are you in *the joy of the Lord*? Sometimes we can conjure up human happiness, but only God can give us joy. It's time to embrace your joy. It is available for the asking!

What Goes Around, Comes Around
Life Lesson #52

I'M SURE OUR DAUGHTERS WISH THEY HAD A DOLLAR for every time they've heard me say, "What goes around, comes around." I've used the phrase often when trying to convey to them our words and our actions have consequences.

The Bible states this principle in a crisp, clear way:

Do not be deceived: God cannot be mocked. A man reaps what he sows (Galatians 6:7).

Paul used an agricultural analogy to speak to this fact of life--we reap what we sow. "What goes around, comes around."

As I thought about this Life Lesson, I realized an amazing number of verses in the Bible speak directly to the sowing and reaping principle. I'd like to categorize them by quoting Dr. Charles Stanley: "You reap what you sow, more than you sow, later than you sow."

1. **You reap what you sow**.
   Before the days of hybrid seeds and GMOs (Genetically Modified Organisms), farmers could be sure whatever seed they sowed would produce the corresponding plant. For example, watermelon seeds produced watermelons; pumpkin seeds produced pumpkins; etc.

   In recent years, I've heard farmers say they no longer have access to non-GMO seeds. In the good old days, seeds from the previous year's crops were planted to produce the next harvest.

   It was a principle of life that what you put in the ground would come up from the ground. It is also true in life that what you put into your life, and into the lives of others, brings forth a harvest of like kind you will be forced to reap one day.

If you sow goodness, you will reap goodness. However, if you sow evil, you will reap evil.

The choice is ours. Either: *Peacemakers who sow in peace reap a harvest of righteousness* (James 3:18). Or: *As I have observed, those who plow evil and those who sow trouble reap it* (Job 4:8).

I think if we take time to consider the future consequences of what we say and do, we will be more careful about what we sow into our lives and the lives of others.

2. **You reap more than you sow.**
   Agriculturally, a single seed that sprouts will yield numerous other seeds. Farmers know this fact and keep it in mind while planting.

The same is true in life. When we sow good seeds, it is amazing how the good multiplies and blesses us and others:

Give, and it will be given to you. A good measure, pressed down, shaken together and running over, will be poured into your lap. For with the measure you use, it will be measured to you (Luke 6:38).

Unfortunately, the opposite is also true. Sowing bad things leads to reaping bad things abundantly:

Sow righteousness for yourselves, reap the fruit of unfailing love, and break up your unplowed ground; for it is time to seek the Lord, until he comes and showers his righteousness on you. But you have planted wickedness, you have reaped evil, you have eaten the fruit of deception

> *because you have depended on your own strength and on your many warriors* (Hosea 10:12-13).

3. You reap later than you sow.

Even though agriculturally most seeds planted one season produce a crop that same season, in life we may not see the harvest for some time. But, reaping day will come!

Sometimes people think because they don't see immediate results of their evil doing, they have escaped any consequences. However, the harvest may even come in a totally different season of life:

> *They will eat the fruit of their ways and be filled with the fruit of their schemes* (Proverbs 1:31)..

I believe that's why the Bible urges us not to give up planting good seeds, even when we don't see immediate results:

> *Let us not become weary in doing good, for at the proper time we will reap a harvest if we do not give up. Therefore, as we have opportunity, let us do good to all people, especially to those who belong to the family of believers* (Galatians 6:9-10).

In God's due season, we face consequences of our willful decisions. Most of the time, people around us can tell by our harvest what kind of seeds we've planted.

A little boy helped his father plant corn. The boy was supposed to come behind his father and put a couple of beans in with the corn kernels for the bean vines to wrap around the corn stalks as they grew.

However, the little boy wanted to hurry and finish so he could play. He began dropping a handful of beans in with the corn rather than the couple he was supposed to plant. As the garden grew, it was obvious to all who saw it what had happened. Only a few corn stalks survived the heavy bean vines that resulted from the little boy's disobedience. I know this story is true. Wayne was the little boy in the story!

Will you be filled with joy or remorse on harvest day? Remember: "We reap what we sow," and "What goes around, comes around."

THERE'S NO PLACE LIKE HOME
LIFE LESSON #53

As I WRITE THIS, WE ARE MAKING PREPARATIONS for the arrival of Hurricane Irma, the strongest Atlantic hurricane on record. The path of the storm fluctuates with almost each update, so we do not know what to expect. I look around our house and wonder what it will look like in a few days. Will it even be standing?

These questions cause me to think anew about the meaning of "home." You see, whether or not the house makes it through the storm, with God's help, our home will survive.

I love the following verse because it teaches us the things that make a house a home are not material things at all--they are matters of the heart:

By wisdom a house is built, and through understanding it is established; through knowledge its rooms are filled with rare and beautiful treasures (Proverbs 24:3-4).

Wisdom, understanding, and **knowledge** are God's perfect building materials. Recently, I thought about all the places I've lived. I've moved 16 times in my lifetime, and I've lived in everything from a row house in Baltimore, Maryland to a Mobile Home Villa in Myrtle Beach, SC. I've lived in a dormitory, a single rented upstairs room, an apartment, very small houses, and nice, larger houses. I've lived in an inner city neighborhood, on a mountainside, at the beach, in suburban areas, and in the country.

Some of the places I've lived were beautiful. Others were only beautiful after renovations. Thankfully, God allows me to look beyond what *is* to what *can be.*

So, one of the greatest Life Lessons I've learned is this: A house does not make a home. Home is much more than a mere house. I guess you could say, "a house houses a home."

One thing has been true in each house where I lived: *there's no place like home!* Before I married, home was my parents, James and Jeri Clary, and my sister, Lynn. After I married, home was Wayne and our daughters, Meri Beth and Molly. As I walked into each house in which I lived, I felt something that's hard to put into words: warmth, joy of being with family members and friends, comfort, completeness, and satisfaction.

So, how can we build the best home possible using the building materials God instructs us to use? I searched the scriptures for some answers I hope will be meaningful to you. They were to me.

The first building material--the foundation--is **wisdom.** True wisdom, can only come from God. Godly wisdom not only secures a home, but also it supports the home through the changing seasons of life.

But the wisdom that comes from heaven is first of all pure; then peace-loving, considerate, submissive, full of mercy and good fruit, impartial and sincere (James 3:17).

Isn't that beautiful? Just look at the attributes of godly wisdom: purity, peace, consideration, submissiveness, mercy, goodness, impartiality and sincerity. Only they can insure home will be the most loved place of all!

The second building material is **understanding.** *And he* [God] *said to the human race, 'The fear* [reverence for] *of the Lord--that is wisdom, and to shun evil is understanding'* (Job 28:28). A home constructed with reverence for God and one that shuns evil will endure. In addition, *the one who has knowledge uses words with restraint, and whoever has understanding is even-tempered* (Proverbs 27:27). Understanding leads to self-control when relating to others.

The final building material is **knowledge.** *Teach me knowledge and good judgment, for I trust your commands* (Psalm 119:66). No matter how beautiful a house may be, the furnishings make it come alive. God's commands and promises are the *rare and beautiful treasures* (Proverbs 24:4) that fill the rooms.

No home is perfect, just as no family is perfect. However, with **wisdom, understanding**, and **knowledge**, we can build toward our eternal home which is perfect.

As we renovated the house where we presently live, we took magic markers and covered the sub-floors and unpainted walls with scripture. It was fun to choose Bible verses that would be appropriate for each room.

Our granddaughter, Mazi Grace, was in kindergarten with the son of Andre' Davis, a former NFL player. I helped with the end-of-the-year class party at the Davis' home, and a scripture plaque in the kitchen caught my attention. When I commented on it to Andre', he led me to their beautiful, double stair-cased foyer and showed me the scriptures stenciled all around the foyer ceiling. They also had written scriptures on their sub-floors and unpainted walls. He then walked into their family room and stood in a marked spot as he explained, "We have a Bible underneath this spot because this is the center of the house."

Wow! I realized the owners of that beautiful mansion had found the biblical secret of building a "home" - **wisdom**, **understanding**, and **knowledge**.

As it has turned out, we only got the fringe of Hurricane Irma, and our house is unharmed. So is our home. I am thankful, because truly, *there is no place like home*!

"Red and Yellow, Black and White..."
Life Lesson #54

A SONG I LEARNED AS A CHILD CONTAINS THE essence of love:

> *Jesus loves the little children;*
> *All the children of the world.*
> *Red and yellow, black and white,*
> *All are precious in His sight.*
> *Jesus loves the little children of the world.*
> (Composer: George Frederick Root Lyrics: Clare Herbert Woolston)

One of the greatest Life Lessons I've ever learned is people are people regardless of the color of their skin. Period.

I've lived through the days of segregation and the days of integration. I've lived through the days of social injustice and through the days of affirmative action and other man-made plans to try to create a form of equality. I've lived through riots and peace marches. Whew! I've seen fighting, arguing, venomous prejudices, and scriptural misquotes from different cultures trying to prove they are more acceptable than other cultures.

The truth is there is only one race in the world--the human race. Even though there are different ethnicities and cultures, religions and creeds, the fact remains that all humans are a part of the human race. Our humanity unites us, unless we let it divide us.

- **Bottom line: God equally loves each person He ever created!** It is hard for us to imagine such pure love since our love is biased by many different influences. God's love is just, and He does not show favoritism [prejudice].
  Then Peter began to speak: 'I now realize how true it is that God does not show favoritism, but accepts from every nation the one who fears him and does what is right' (Acts 34-35).

- **We show favoritism to cultures we feel most comfortable among.** **However, the Bible admonishes that if we are Christians, we should replace our favoritism with God's love.**

  My brothers and sisters, believers in our glorious Lord Jesus Christ must not show favoritism (James 2:1).

- **When we are focused on Christ and serving Him, our prejudices fade in the light of His glory.** As Christ becomes our *all in all,* reaching the people of the world with His love becomes our magnificent obsession.

  Here there is no Gentile or Jew, circumcised or uncircumcised, barbarian, Scythian, slave or free, but Christ is all, and is in all (Colossians 3:11).

While doing mission work Wayne and I have been blessed time and again by the gracious hospitality of people from other cultures. I often envision the faces of people across the world with whom we've had the opportunity of sharing God's love. I pray for them and wonder how they are doing. I remember moments shared over meals, or in worship services. Our lives are enriched by knowing them.

Several years ago, we worked in Philadelphia with the youth from our church. My group was assigned to a children's park. The park had an amazing story. A group of mothers/grandmothers had reclaimed that city park from the drug dealers in the area.

Every day they went to the park to clean it and make it safe for the neighborhood children. Every night the drug gangs trashed the park. The next morning the mother/grandmother brigade went back to the park and cleaned it up again. That night the drug gangs trashed it. This went on for almost a year before the drug gangs left the area.

As I worked in the park, I met a lady who was walking three dogs through the park. In a short time, we realized how much we had in common. We both had taught special education, we both had a degree in remedial reading, and we both had been itinerant teachers. I asked about her faith. The Holy Spirit had prepared her heart through recent reading she had done and things she had experienced. I asked if she felt the desire to open her heart and receive God's salvation through Jesus. She readily agreed.

At that exact moment, a big mongrel dog galloped across the park, her dogs lunged forward to chase it, and they broke loose from her. We ran to catch them. I yelled for the youth to help. I remember begging God to intervene because she seemed so ready to receive Him.

The youth returned the dogs to her. About that time the bus arrived to carry our group back to the college where we were staying. I turned to my new friend and asked if she remembered what we were about to do before the dogs ran off. She said, "Yes, let's pray."

We prayed, and she accepted God's salvation! Through tears I said, "Now we're sisters."

She laughed and put her brown arm against my arm and said, "I don't see how we could be sisters."

I assured her that the color of our skin didn't matter because our hearts were connected through God's love. Then I said, "Besides, I'm part Cherokee anyway."

She looked shocked and said, "So am I, but I've never told anyone. As a black woman, I was already a minority, so I didn't want to add anything else."

I climbed aboard the bus, and we waved goodbye through the window. Indeed, red and yellow, black and white, *we* really *are* precious in His sight!

❈

GOD'S PATTERNS
LIFE LESSON #55

In the beginning was the Word, and the Word was with God, and the Word was God (John 1:1).

GOD IS THE GREAT CREATOR, DESIGNER, ENGINEER, Architect, Decorator, Artist...He's the great I Am! One of my favorite things to do is look for patterns tucked away in scripture passages. It always thrills me to find a pattern that expands a theme and connects it with other themes in the Bible.

For example, a beautiful pattern is found through the names listed in the genealogy in Genesis 5. The names, in their exact order in the Bible, present a salvation message. From Adam to Noah, the names translate, "Man, [was] Appointed, Mortal sorrow; [but] The Blessed God, shall come down, teaching. His death shall bring, the despairing, rest (or comfort.)" Isn't that amazing?

One of the most thrilling patterns occurred to me as I mopped the floor. I reflected on the genealogy in Genesis 5, and I suddenly wondered if the order of the days of creation had a special message.

I dropped the mop, ran to my Bible, and looked up the creation narrative in Genesis 1:1 – 2:3. Tears flowed as I realized the days of creation sequentially show us how to live: spirit, soul, and body! It contains the pattern for holiness, happiness, and health.

Day One	Light and Happiness (The Hebrew word used here for Light, "owr," must be coupled with happiness to be complete. God's Light is the way to happiness.)
Second Day	Waters were separated making the atmosphere and the water on the earth. Air (breathing) and water (drinking) in that order are essential for our health.
Third Day	Dry land and plant life

The plants are listed in three categories: vegetables, seeds [seeds, nuts, whole grains, and legumes], and fruit. Modern research proves the validity of eating the plants in this order.

Fourth Day	Sun, moon, and stars The creations of the fourth day ensure activity and night-time sleep (day and night), signs (special Holy observances), and seasons (food throughout the year.)
Fifth Day	Fish of the sea and fowl of the air If we are going to eat meat, clean fish and unpolluted fowl are the most healthful choices.
Sixth Day	Land animals and man Of the land animals listed, only the cattle category is considered healthy. The creeping things and beasts of the field are predators.
Seventh Day	Sabbath The Sabbath is a special day designed for rest, holiness, and joy.

I was asked to develop the above pattern into a book. The Creation Diet came out in 2006, and currently, I am re-writing and abridging it. The title also will change since it is a lifestyle rather than a diet. However, the principles, as listed above, will still be the foundation of the book. I find it amazing the first verses of the Bible show us how to live and be healthy even today!

Another pattern in scripture and historical writings has to do with our obedience and/or disobedience to God. Of course, the following events happened in different years, but they all happened on the 17th day of the Hebrew month of Nisan:

Noah's ark came to rest on Mt. Ararat; the Hebrews entered Egypt; the Israelites passed through the parted Red Sea; the Israelites entered the Promised Land and ate of the fruit; the walls of Jericho fell; Esther helped save the Hebrews from annihilation; and Jesus rose from the dead!

Conversely, the following events occurred on the 9th day of the Hebrew month of Av:

The children of Israel did not trust God when they got to the Promised Land and, as a consequence, God decreed that most of them would remain in the wilderness; the first temple was destroyed in 586 BC; the second temple was destroyed in 70 AD.

God's Holy Word *is* amazing! Throughout its pages, God included many fascinating patterns. Only He could inspire a book so wonderful. It is the Living Word. Enjoy time in His Word as you explore its pages and look for His amazing patterns!

TRUTH OR CONSEQUENCES
LIFE LESSON #56

All your words are true; all your righteous laws are eternal
(Psalm 119:160).

OUR NATION ONCE AGAIN IS REELING FROM THE shock of a senseless shooting massacre, this one in Las Vegas, Nevada. Fifty-nine people died, and almost 500 people were injured.

During that same time, I had the privilege of spending time with two close friends who were dying, one in a Hospice House and the other in a hospital. I could tell their deaths would be close to the same time. They died one hour apart in the wee hours Sunday morning.

So, in the face of life and death, I sought God about the next Life Lesson I should share. Honestly, I waited to write this one because in the midst of the circumstances, I had a hard time discerning what to say. I'd sit down to write (in fact, I started several times), but I realized whatever I wrote would just be my own words, and I didn't want that.

I wanted to be open to the Holy Spirit's guidance with what I wrote. So, I pray these next few Life Lessons will be especially meaningful to you. They are, I believe, the crux of what our lives are all about—or should be.

Most of you know me. If not personally, you know me through the Life Lessons or through other people. So I think I can safely say you know I try to be an open-minded person who respects the opinions of others. However, I already know what I write in these next few lessons may be offensive to some people, and that is not my intention at all.

But, I believe we have allowed relativism to rule our lives for so long, our world has gotten completely out of control. For many of you reading this, your personal worlds also have spun out of control.

So how do we get from where we are to where we should be as a person, as a nation, as a world? Is there any place to stand that is such a firm foundation we can camp out there through the storms and changing seasons of life?

I am here to say unequivocally, "Yes, there is!" But to get there, we must re-think the theory so pervasive in our world today that "all truth is relative." It's not. Absolute truths *do* exist, and until we realize that, we will keep making up our own definitions of truth based on our personal opinions about different situations.

Now, I realize it sounds like I'm preaching, but I can assure you Wayne is the preacher in our family, not I. However, I am passionate about what I am sharing, so please forgive me if I appear to jump on a soapbox to present it.

Truth created the world, and Truth sustains the world. I confess one of the reasons truth is so important to me is because I went through a painful search for truth in college. I was a Christian, but when I studied Comparative Religions, I could see areas of what I considered truth in other religions too, and I became confused about my own beliefs.

So, I secretly began a search for truth. I looked at the things I had been taught as a child and youth, and I began questioning them. Why did I believe them? Couldn't I just take the truths from a lot of different religions and be okay?

Let me say here I am very grateful I went through this troubling time. I now know *why* I believe what I believe.

Yes, most religions do have areas of truth in them. Most have admirable lessons, especially on how to treat others. However, I could see in them many questions about truth--but few answers. Most believed in reincarnation, hoping if they didn't find truth in this life, they might have another chance.

Once I recognized the uncertainties of life after death in the various religions, I tightly embraced my Judeo-Christian roots because I realized anew that from the beginning to the end of the Bible (in the original languages), *truth* is presented. Why would I search for truth anywhere else, when I had held it in my hands each time I opened the Bible? It was then up to me to apply the truth I found in its pages.

God's Word is Truth (John 17:17).
Jesus is Truth (John 14:6).
Truth will make us free (John 8:32).
Truth leads to eternal life (I John 5:20).

As I've said before, Satan's fiercest weapon against us is the distortion of truth. Let's put an end to Satan's tactics. Man-made relative truths are exactly that—man-made. Let's come to the Source of absolute truth in the world! Every area of our lives will be affected by our decision.

Please stay with me! In the next lesson you will be presented with the four questions that could change your life forever. I love you, fellow Seekers!

AND THE ANSWER IS...
LIFE LESSON #57

Nothing in all creation is hidden from God's sight. Everything is uncovered before the eyes of him to whom we must give account (Hebrews 4:13).

IT GIVES ME GREAT ASSURANCE TO REALIZE GOD IS omniscient (all-knowing), and He has the answers to all my questions. Nothing is hidden from Him.

Researchers say there are four universal questions each person asks in life:

Who am I?
Where did I come from?
What is the meaning of life?
Where will I go when I die?

We live in an ever-changing world, yet I think we all will agree those universal questions remain. In this changing world, one of the most fascinating, yet personally frustrating, changes to me is technology.

However, one of the tools I appreciate is the Siri on my cell phone, especially when I drive. I can push a little button to get information, and I don't have to look down at the screen.

But, my Siri sometimes has a hard time understanding my Southern accent (i.e., "well" is written "whale" in texts), *and* she gets an attitude for no apparent reason. And I'm even nice to her by saying "please" and "thank you."

So, I decided to ask my Siri the four universal questions to see what she would say. The following are her answers:

Who am I? Siri: "You're asking me, Joy?" (Notice the attitude!)
Where did I come from? Siri: "Interesting question, Joy."
What is the meaning of life? Siri: "That's easy...it's a philosophical question concerning the purpose and significance of life or existence in general." (I didn't think that was easy.)
Where will I go when I die? Siri: "No comment."

Sadly, if we asked people around us question #4, we would probably get answers similar to Siri's "no comment" (i.e., "I *hope* I go to heaven").

Is it possible to have answers for these questions? *Since nothing in all creation is hidden from God*, let's look at the answers He gives us through scripture.

The first three can be found in the following single passage:

'Bring My sons from afar, and My daughters from the ends of the earth--everyone who is called by My name, whom I have created for My glory; I have formed him, yes, I have made him' (Isaiah 43:6b-7 NKJV).

Who am I? We are creations of God, but we have the potential of being sons or daughters of the Heavenly Father: *Yet to all who did receive him, to those who believed in his name, he gave the right to become children of God* (John 1:12).

Where did I come from? God tells us He *created* us, *formed* us, and *made* us!

What is the meaning of life? God says we were created for His glory. Glorifying Him (showing the world how wonderful He is) is the key to meaning in life. We were born to reflect His glory.

Where will I go when I die? Jesus assures us in John 14:2-6 there is a special place [called Heaven] available to us through Him. We don't have to *hope* to go to heaven, we can solidify the decision that assures us of heaven: *It is a trustworthy statement: For if we died with Him, we will also live with Him* (2 Timothy 2:11).

I'd like to conclude this Life Lesson with a very personal experience that profoundly impacted my life.

My sister, Lynn, and I were blessed with wonderful parents. Our father was one of the most intelligent men I've ever known. For years he was a television repairman, but he realized computers were the wave of the future, so he was back in college at age seventy-seven learning to fix computers. (May I brag a little? He was making straight A's.)

Daddy experienced a brain aneurysm rupture one Saturday morning, and it changed our lives forever. He was in the hospital for six weeks and for several of those weeks he was able to communicate with us. However, after a month, another bleed occurred, and he was left with no brain activity or muscle movement—only the involuntary brain stem activities of heartbeat and breathing.

We as a family were gathered around his bed on the morning of his death. I looked at his hand as I held it, and I thought of how hard his hands had worked for his family, how his hands could seemingly build and repair anything, how his hands could comfort and bring a sense of security.

Suddenly his hand moved and almost slipped out of my hand. I immediately looked up at his face as muscle movement returned. He got an expression on his face almost as if to say, "What is this?" Then he smiled, and he smiled again even bigger, and the third and final time he smiled one of the broadest smiles I'd ever seen, and we knew he was with God whom he loved dearly. The presence of the Holy Spirit was so real in the room, through tears we all spontaneously sang, "Holy, Holy, Holy."

Have *you* found your answers to the questions of life and eternal life?

THE ONE TRUE GOD
LIFE LESSON #58

*And we know that the Son of God has come and has given us
an understanding, that we may know Him who is true; and
we are in Him who is true, in His Son Jesus Christ. This is the
true God and eternal life* (I John 5:20 NKJV).

WE LIVE IN A VERY DIVERSE WORLD. IN ADDITION TO
various religions, "universalism" and "pluralism" seem to pervade the
thinking of a growing number of people. Universalism teaches that it doesn't
matter what you believe. Pluralism teaches that it doesn't matter what religion you adhere to or what the belief system of that religion is. The idea of
one true God is rejected.

However, God is very specific throughout scripture He is the one true
God, and He is the way to heaven. The following are but a few examples of
how God explains who He is:

He has always been (Isaiah 43:10-13).
Indeed, before the day was, I am He...(Isaiah 43:13 NKJV).

There is no God except Him (Isaiah 46:9-10).
...For I am God, and there is no other... (Isaiah 46:9).

Any other "god" is manmade (Isaiah 45:20-23 NKJV).
*They have no knowledge, who carry the wood of their carved image, and pray
to a god that cannot save* (Isaiah 45:20 NKJV).

**Only He can prophesy. He tells the end from the beginning, and every-
thing He says comes true** (Isaiah 48:3-5 NKJV).
*I have declared the former things from the beginning; they went forth from My
mouth, and I caused them to hear it. Suddenly I did them, and they came to
pass* (Isaiah 48:3 NKJV).

Only He can save (Isaiah 43:10-13).
I, even I, am the Lord, and besides Me there is no savior (Isaiah 43:11 NKJV).

I have noticed that there are two major issues that seem to block many people from accepting the fact there is only one true God. Those issues are the following:

1. What about those who have never heard of this one true God?
2. What about children or mentally disabled?

Those who have never heard:
We read the following in Romans 1:20: *For since the creation of the world, His invisible attributes, His eternal power and divine nature, have been clearly seen, being understood through what has been made, so that they are without excuse.* I believe as people respond to what they can know about God He gives further knowledge of Himself.

On our way to a mission trip to Russia, Wayne and I shared about God's plan of salvation with our Russian flight attendant. She accepted joyfully and told us somehow in her heart she knew this, but she didn't know the whole story or what to call Him. Isn't God amazing?

God also speaks to people through dreams and visions. I taught at a technical college, and a young Vietnamese lady came to me with some questions. She said when she was a young girl, a bleeding man suddenly appeared to her in her yard. She said, "Oh, Sir, you are hurt. I will help you." She ran inside to get some rags, but when she returned he was gone.

Years later, after an amazing escape from Vietnam, she saw a crucifix on the outside of a church in Thailand, and she somehow knew that was the man she had seen in her yard. She asked me, "Who was that man, and why was He bleeding?"

This young lady and her Buddhist husband both accepted Christ! God had prepared her heart years before, and through the years He revealed to her who He is in different ways through various circumstances.

Children and Mentally Disabled:
A scriptural principle shows us God takes care of those who are young (or mentally young.) The young people who did not have a full understanding of good or evil were allowed to enter the Promised Land, even though those who rebelled against God were not allowed to do so: *Moreover, your little*

ones whom you said would become a prey, and your sons, who this day have no understanding of good or evil, shall enter there, and I will give it to them and they shall possess it (Deuteronomy 1:39 NKJV).

I'm fascinated with the stories that surround the sinking of the Titanic. Even though the great ship sailed from Southampton, England, the White Star Line, which built the Titanic, was headquartered in Liverpool, England.

The days following the tragic accident and sinking of the ship were chaotic as families tried to get word about their loved ones who were onboard. White Star had a large billboard on the outside of their office, and they would add names to the boards daily.

Two columns were on the board with the headings, "Known to be saved," and "Known to be lost."

With all my heart I desire for you to be on the "Known to be saved" list, with the complete assurance of salvation through the *one true God*! If you are not, please ask God for the faith to believe He is who He says He is.

FAITH
LIFE LESSON #59

Now faith is confidence in what we hope for and assurance about what we do not see (Hebrews 11:1).

MANY OF OUR FAMILY BIRTHDAY CELEBRATIONS occur during autumn, so it's a time of gift-giving and fun. Shopping is *not* one of my favorite things to do! I know most women reading this are thinking, "What?" However, I do like to try to think of gifts people would enjoy. Sometimes they are useful gifts, and sometimes they are just frivolous gifts to make the recipient feel pampered.

Because gift-giving is on my mind right now, I want to share three of God's greatest gifts to us--faith, hope, and love. We will look at each of these over the next few lessons. However, the amazing thing about these gifts is they increase the more you use them. You can't use them up, because they actually grow in strength and value as you use them.

Our youth choir in Raleigh sang a song Wayne wrote entitled "Exercise Your Faith." The basis of the song was just as we exercise our bodies to grow strong, we must exercise our faith to grow strong spiritually.

So, exactly what is faith? If I may paraphrase our opening verse (Hebrews 11:1), I believe faith is "believing God is working for good in our lives even when we can't see how He is accomplishing it."

A few of the most important things I've learned about faith in my life are the following:

Faith leads us to a relationship with God.
Therefore, since we have been justified through faith, we have peace with God through our Lord Jesus Christ (Romans 5:1).

Faith comes from God.
...Do not think of yourself more highly than you ought, think of yourself with sober judgment, in accordance with the faith God has distributed to each of you (Romans 12:3b). Faith is both a gift of the Holy Spirit (I Corinthians 12:9) and a fruit of the Holy Spirit (Galatians 5:22).

Faith pleases God.
And without faith it is impossible to please God, because anyone who comes to him must believe that he exists and that he rewards those who earnestly seek him (Hebrews 11:6).

Do you see the beauty of this? God gives us faith so we can believe He exists, and then He gives us the gift of faith once we come into a relationship with Him. He gives us all the faith we need to make it through life in a way that pleases Him!

Faith is measured by God in His own way.
...Truly I tell you, if you have faith as small as a mustard seed, you can say to this mountain, 'Move from here to there,' and it will move. Nothing will be impossible for you (Matthew 17:21).

Faith, when tested, produces perseverance that leads to spiritual maturity.
Consider it pure joy, my brothers and sisters, whenever you face trials of many kinds, because you know that testing of your faith produces perseverance. Let perseverance finish its work so that you may be mature and complete, not lacking anything (James 1:2-4).

It's difficult to *consider it joy* when circumstances test our faith, but when we persevere in our faith, we grow in spiritual maturity. And, isn't growing to be like Jesus the goal of our faith?

Truthfully, with the confusion in the world around us, and the confusion we experience in our own lives, the only way to increase our faith is to stay focused on *who* God is. Reading His Word teaches us His character and increases our faith: *So then faith comes by hearing, and hearing by the word of God* (Romans 10:17 NKJV).

When I try to figure out how God is working in certain situations, I find it takes my focus away from who He is. I attempt to figure out what He is doing instead of trusting He has promised to use everything that happens to me for good in my life (Romans 8:28).

When I simply let God *be* God, I find my faith increases: *'For my thoughts are not your thoughts, neither are your ways my ways,' declares the Lord. 'As the heavens are higher than the earth, so are my ways higher than your ways and my thoughts than your thoughts'* (Isaiah 55:8-9). One acrostic defines FAITH as "Forsaking All I Trust Him," and that saying puts it in the right perspective.

Let's commit to exercise our faith every day we live, and in doing so, we will also please our wonderful Lord!

HOPE
LIFE LESSON #60

Therefore, being justified by faith, we have peace with God through our Lord Jesus Christ: By whom also we have access by faith into this grace wherein we stand, and rejoice in hope of the glory of God. And not only so, but we glory in tribulations also: knowing that tribulations worketh patience; And patience, experience; and experience, hope (Romans 5:1-4 KJV).

TODAY WE CONTINUE OUR LOOK AT THREE OF GOD'S greatest gifts--faith, hope, and love--as written in I Corinthians 13:13. Hope is listed next to love!

One of my favorite childhood memories is of my father creating treasure maps for my friends and me (and for my sister, Lynn, when she was old enough.) Sometimes he would hide a surprise at the end of the game, but often he just left a note congratulating us for following the clues.

I believe that childhood game helped me learn to look for patterns in God's Word. I am always excited when I see pieces of the puzzle coming together, and I find the treasure hidden in a particular verse or passage.

Recently, I found a hidden gem in the opening passage about hope. The teacher in me enjoys developing acrostics to use as learning tools, so this one on how to have HOPE is based on the opening passage from Romans 5:1-4:

H - Hold onto your faith.

The first two verses tell us *faith* is how we gain access to *hope*. Once we, through faith, accept God's gift of grace, we naturally rejoice in the hope of God's glory.

In your quest for hope, hold on to whatever amount of faith you currently have. Remember from the last Life Lesson the more you use your faith, the more it grows. Also, God has His own way of measuring your faith. If faith the size of a tiny mustard seed can move a mountain, whatever level of faith you currently have will be used by God to help you realize His hope.

Even if you are questioning; even if you are doubting; confess the faith you do have, and ask for enough faith to access hope.

To me, one of the most honest confessions/prayers in the Bible was uttered by the father of a demon possessed boy. When the father said to Jesus, '*if you can help,*' Jesus questioned the man's use of the word "*if*."

Immediately the boy's father exclaimed, 'I do believe; help me overcome my unbelief!' (Mark 9:24) God knows you and loves you no matter how strong or weak your faith may be at any given moment.

O - Open your heart and mind to what God sees as best for you rather than what you want. Sometimes the reason the things we hope for do not happen is because we are hoping for the wrong things. You probably remember Garth Brooks' popular song, "Unanswered Prayers." In it he thanks God for not answering his prayers in the way he wanted concerning what he now realizes was the wrong girl. He concludes, "Some of God's greatest gifts are unanswered prayers."

P - Persevere with patience.
Our focal passage goes on to say the reason we can rejoice in tribulations is because they help us learn patience. In many situations there is nothing we can do, and we have to wait on God. That waiting helps us grow in patience.

Wayne says God answers prayer in three ways: "yes," "no," or "wait and see." The "wait and see" is sometimes even more difficult than "no," but it is during those times patience develops.

E - Experience [some translations use the word "character"]
The last verse assures us our patience produces experience, and the experience we gain from patience leads to *hope*.

I've tried to be transparent in the Life Lessons, often sharing with you sorrows and/or triumphs I've experienced, and what I learned from them. I must admit most of the time, hope came easily in my life, and I had taken it for granted.

Then, last summer when our granddaughter became sick and there were seemingly no answers for what was happening, I began to feel hopeless. I've also heard Wayne say in sermons, "If you feel hopeless, you begin to feel helpless." (See, I do listen to my husband's sermons:) And the hopeless, helpless feeling was awful.

Then, through an amazing sequence of events, we were led to a specialist in New Jersey who was able to help, and she is a happy, healthy girl again. The hope he offered was priceless.

As painful as the experience was, I'm now more aware of hope than ever. The hope I had come to take for granted, I now try to nurture and help it grow. After all, hope is the *anchor for the soul* (Hebrews 6:19).

If you are struggling to find hope, please use the principles in the acrostic above to help you experience God's beautiful gift of *hope*.

This is my sincere prayer for you:

May the God of hope fill you with all joy and peace as you trust in him, so that you may overflow with hope by the power of the Holy Spirit (Romans 15:13). Amen.

LOVE—THE GREATEST GIFT
LIFE LESSON #61

And now these three remain: faith, hope and love. But the greatest of these is love (I Corinthians 13:13).

"TAKE AWAY LOVE AND OUR EARTH IS A TOMB."
Robert Browning

I'm sure we could agree "love" is such a broad concept, we could talk about it every day for the rest of our lives and never exhaust its ramifications. I'm convinced love is one of the two greatest motivators in the world. I believe fear is the other. But thankfully...*perfect love drives out fear*...(I John 4:18).

We use the word love in many different ways without distinguishing what we mean. For example, with one breath we say we love God. In the next moment, we say we love Hallmark Christmas Movies. We love our favorite recipe, but also we love our family and friends. We love a brisk walk in the fresh air, and we love our favorite scripture verse.

The Greeks have helped us categorize love. They have several words for love, four of which are fairly well-known. At least two of them are found in the New Testament.

Eros--passionate love usually with sensual desire. It also has been described as romantic love.

Storge'--natural affection like that felt by parents for their children. Storge' is used most often to describe relationships within the family.

"It's easy to love the people from far away. It is not always easy to love those close to us. It is easier to give a cup of rice to relieve hunger than to relieve the loneliness and pain of someone unloved in our own home. Bring love into your home for this is where our love for each other must start."—Mother Teresa

Phileo--love between friends better known as friendship. Philadelphia is even called, "The City of Brotherly [friendship] Love."

Agape'--self-sacrificing, giving love to all. Agape' has been referred to as unconditional love. God gives us this kind of love to share with others.

I've heard we should "like things and love people." Perhaps that's true, because to my knowledge even the Greeks did not have a word to describe a love for *things*.

So, how do *you* define love? Please take a moment and consider your answer to this question. Your answer could change the course of your life.

The wisdom of children amazes me. I find myself constantly asking our grandchildren, "How do you know that?"

Several years ago, a group of professional people surveyed children 4-8 years of age. They asked them one simple question, "What does love mean?" (www.rogerknapp.com) Their answers astounded me, so I wanted to share them with you as well as some valuable points I found in them. Enjoy!

Love originated from God, and He wants us to share it with others.
"There are two kinds of love. Our love. God's love. But God makes both kinds of them." Jenny--age 8

Love is not about things, it's about people.
"Love is what's in the room with you at Christmas if you stop opening presents and listen." Bobby—age 7

Love should be expressed.
"You really shouldn't say 'I love you' unless you mean it. But if you mean it, you should say it a lot. People forget." Jessica—age 8

Love desires the best for another person.
"Love is when you go out to eat and give somebody most of your French Fries without making them give you any of theirs." Chrissy—age 6

Love is a safe place to put your heart.
"When someone loves you, the way they say your name is different. You know your name is safe in their mouth." Billy—age 4

Love can be tested which gives you the opportunity to strengthen and protect it.
"If you want to learn to love better, you should start with a friend who you hate." Nikka—age 6

And now these three remain: faith, hope and love. But the greatest of these is love (I Corinthians 13:13).

I hope you've learned from our Life Lessons on faith, hope, and love. Wayne tells how some years ago he thought about the above verse and wondered why the Bible says love is the greatest of the three. Then God revealed to him some day--when we are in God's presence--our faith will be realized. We will be with the One in whom we've placed our trust. Our hope will be realized. We will be with the ones we've been hoping to see again. But love is eternal, and it will never end!

In the words of little Jessica, age 8, "...if you mean it ['I love you'], you should say it a lot. People forget." I don't want you to forget, so let me remind you as readers, "I love you!"

TAKE MY HAND, PRECIOUS LORD
LIFE LESSON #62

I, the Lord, have called you in righteousness; I will take hold of your hand. I will keep you and make you to be a covenant for the people and a light for the Gentiles [nations] (Isaiah 42:6).

I SHARED IN AN EARLIER POST THAT ISAIAH 42:6 IS my favorite Bible verse. I can still remember how it thrilled my young heart the first time I read it as a child. The thought of God holding my hand was one of the most beautiful things I could imagine. I would sometimes lift my little hand above my head to make it easier for God to take hold of it, and I'd walk around holding His hand in mine. (To my sister, Lynn, I want to say if you ever saw me doing that--now you know why.)

This verse still thrills me! As a child, I did not understand the second part of the verse about "covenants" and "Gentiles," ["nations"], so I claimed Isaiah 42:6a as my favorite verse. Little did I realize at this present stage of my life, the second part of the verse would be unfolding as Wayne and I try to share the gospel (*a light to the nations*) through various ways in different parts of the world through *Diversified Ministries*.

I looked up the Hebrew word for "keep," and found it means "to guard, protect, maintain." So one aspect of God holding our hand is He guards us, much like parents who take the hand of a child to guard, protect, and lead him or her.

As I looked up other scriptures that speak of God's hand, I realized one of the greatest Life Lessons we can learn is the importance of living our lives holding onto God's hand, and allowing Him to hold ours. The following are but a few of the scriptures that illustrate this amazing point:

God's Hand Works for Our Salvation.
Sing to the Lord a new song, for he has done marvelous things; his right hand and his holy arm have worked salvation for him (Psalm 98:1).

God's Hand Gives Strength.
Wealth and honor come from you; you are the ruler of all things, in your hands are strength and power to exalt and give strength to all (I Chronicles 29:12).

God's Hand Leads.

If I rise on the wings of the dawn, if I settle on the far side of the sea, even there your hand will guide me, your right hand will hold me fast (Psalm 139: 9-10).

God's Hand Does Mighty Things.

Shouts of joy and victory resound in the tents of the righteous: 'The Lord's right hand has done mighty things' (Psalm 118:15).

God's Hand Molds Us.

Yet you, Lord, are our father. We are the clay, you are the potter; we are all the work of your hand (Isaiah 64:8).

God's Hand Shatters the Enemy.

Your right hand, Lord, was majestic in power. Your right hand, Lord, shattered the enemy (Exodus 15:6).

God's Hand Calms Our Fear and Helps Us.

For I am the LORD your God who takes hold of your right hand and says to you, 'Do not fear, I will help you' (Isaiah 41:13).

We will face trials in life. The Bible never promises we won't. But it does promise when we walk hand in hand with God, we can endure and experience victory even in the trials.

Thomas A. Dorsey wrote the music and lyrics to the beautiful song, "Take My Hand, Precious Lord." The song was born out of deep pain when Mr. Dorsey's wife and young child died. For many months his anguish seemed overwhelming. One night he attended an inspirational meeting with some friends. When he got home, he was unable to sleep. As he tossed and turned, the words "Take My Hand..." began to form as he later described it, "like drops of water falling into a deep, calm pond." Thus, one of the best-loved spirituals of all time formed in his mind.

Please read Mr. Dorsey's poignant lyrics as you think of which area of your life you need to hold onto God's hand more tightly.

Precious Lord, take my hand, lead me on, let me stand.
I am tired, I am weak, I am worn.
Thru the storm, thru the night, lead me on to the light.
Take my hand, precious Lord, lead me home.

When my way grows drear, Precious Lord, linger near.
When my life is almost gone.
Hear my cry, hear my call. Hold my hand, lest I fall,
Take my hand, precious Lord, lead me home.

When the darkness appears, and the night draws near.
And the day is past and gone.
At the river I stand. Guide my feet, hold my hand.
Take my hand, precious Lord, and lead me home.

It's All a Journey
Life Lesson #63

A FEW DAYS AGO, A YOUNG FRIEND POSTED A POI-gnant message on Facebook. At this time in her life, she is hurting emotionally. Yet she feels if she's honest about her feelings, her faith might be questioned or judged.

I answered that many of the Life Lessons I've written were learned in the valleys rather than on the mountaintops. I told her, "It's all a journey." As soon as I wrote those words, I felt that saying should be today's Life Lesson, because, really, it *is* all a journey.

- **This amazing journey begins with birth.**
  Before I formed you in the womb, I knew you, before you were born I set you apart... (Jeremiah 1:5).

Some of you were born into ideal circumstances where you were loved and nurtured; others where you were abandoned or neglected; still others where your innate abilities were stifled by controlling parents or siblings.

Whatever your beginning may have been, it is a part of your journey, but it is *not* your whole journey. "Whether or not you were planned on by your parents, you were planned on by God." (Rick Warren) God wants your past to strengthen you rather than cripple you.

- **This amazing journey includes a time to "grow up."**
  When I was a child, I talked like a child, I thought like a child, I reasoned like a child. When I became a man, I put the ways of childhood behind me (I Corinthians 13:11)

Some people fail to progress on the journey because they perpetually expect to be treated like children. Or even worse, they act like children--failing to accept responsibility for themselves and for others in their care. Unfortunately, the journey of life is filled with adults who behave like children and impede the progress of people they could be helping.

On the other hand, even when we grow up, we should never lose our childlike faith, sense of awe, and playfulness. Lyman Coleman says, "To be child-like is to be Christ-like. To be childish is to be selfish."

- **This amazing journey includes a time to gain independence.**
  Remember your Creator in the days of your youth... (Ecclesiastes 12:1).

The teenage years grant us more freedom and responsibility while still under the covering of parents/guardians. I call this the "lollipop to lipstick" age, because most teenagers want freedom, but--whether or not they will admit it--they still need the security of not being totally in charge of their lives.

It breaks my heart to think of some of the things our youth face today as compared to teens a generation ago. The "Happy Days" of sitting on the car hoods laughing and talking with friends at the Tastee-Freeze or Colonial drive-in restaurants (in my home town) were, for the most part, carefree days of fun. As the world changed, it brought alarming temptations to our teens. They need a strong prayer covering during this part of life's journey. Yet it is also during these years, some of the strongest followers of Christ emerge as they seek Him to help them resist the temptations.

- **This amazing journey includes a time to find our purpose(s) in life and flourish.**
  In all your ways acknowledge Him, and He will direct your paths (Proverbs 3:6 NKJV).

From making decisions about education, jobs, careers, mates--to the years of excelling in careers and/or raising families--to reaching an age that allows us to enjoy the fruit of our labors, this amazing journey becomes the sum total of our decisions and choices in life. We look back and wonder, "Where have the years gone?"

- **The end of this amazing journey leads us either to--or away from--our heavenly home.**

...'What no eye has seen, what no ear has heard, and what no human mind has conceived'--the things God has prepared for those who love him... (I Corinthians 2:9).

Not only has God promised to be with us every step of this journey, but also He has prepared a place for us to dwell with Him eternally, and it is more wonderful than anything we have ever seen, heard, or could imagine. Have you accepted His provision to enter this heavenly home?

The following are a few realizations that can help us on this journey:

1. We will make mistakes along the way. We must learn to forgive ourselves and move forward anyway.
2. Sometimes we travel quickly, and sometimes we travel at a snail's pace. Remember: Life is the sum total of all our decisions, and some decisions don't need to be rushed.
3. Each step we take is a part of the journey. Some steps are fun. Others are terrifying. Some are soothing. Others are hurtful. Some are obvious. Others require blind faith.
4. Of utmost importance, we must make the decision to hold onto the hand of God. No matter where we are on the journey, God desires to hold our hand and guide us.

Yes, "it *is* all a journey." So, through the mountains and valleys, enjoy the journey! It passes quickly.

Preparing for the Coming King
Life Lesson #64

...'Prepare the way of the Lord'...(Mark 1:3).

DURING THIS SEASON OF ADVENT, OUR MINDS ARE focused on the King of Glory who left the throne of heaven and visited earth in a lowly stable. The incarnation is confirmed throughout scripture, with historical evidence, and by faith.

Several years ago, I was a co-speaker at a Ladies' Retreat where the theme was "Daughters of the King." My message was, "Preparing for the King."

I provided small stones for the ladies to hold during the session. Their stones represented anything in their lives that hindered them from experiencing "a visit from the King." At whatever point in the retreat they felt release from their hindrances, they were to drop their stones into a pottery container at the front of the sanctuary. I can still remember the thrilling sound of stones being thrown on top of the other stones in the container as people experienced freedom.

God's presence is everywhere, all the time. He is omnipresent. Yet He longs to have special visits with us and give us His blessings. However, we can allow hindrances in our lives that block our ability to feel the presence of the King. In essence, we miss a visit from Him.

In Biblical days, a decree was sent to a village when the king planned to visit. The people rejoiced, because the king brought special gifts when he arrived.

However, the people had to prepare for his coming. If conditions were not conducive for the king to access the people, he would have to pass that village and give the gifts to another village he could reach.

Thus, we see scriptural principles for us to consider during this advent season (and beyond) so our hearts can be open to a Royal visit:

- **The villagers had to remove any rocks or debris that would hinder access (Isaiah 57:14).**
  Is there a sin--obvious or hidden--hindering the King's access to your heart?

- **The villagers had to make the crooked ways straight so the king's entourage could approach (Isaiah 40:3).**
  Are you on the straight road, or have you veered onto crooked paths taking you in the wrong direction?

- **The villagers worked hard to make their village as beautiful as possible for the king (Ephesians 2:10).**
  Are you using your gifts to beautify the world around you for the King?

And now..."the rest of the story."

One night my Bible study teacher taught how the Hebrew letters in the word, "Shalom" (peace) have the following meaning: "Destroy authority attached to chaos." And, isn't that what peace is? In this fallen world we will have chaos, but peace comes when we choose not to let the chaos have authority over us.

That same week, I received an email from my friend, Renee, who was coordinator of the women's retreat I mentioned in the beginning. Renee explained her sister, Christy, had not been able to release her stone at the retreat, and for three months she had carried it or kept it close to her.

Christy's fiancé died in a boating accident on a lake near Charleston, SC. For years, this precious one had carried so much hurt, she was wounded. She knew she had to let it go. She asked Renee and some family members to travel with her to throw her stone in the lake where her fiancé died. Symbolically, she was releasing the conflicted emotions that had been holding her back.

When they returned home, Renee emailed me and said the whole experience was beautiful. Christy walked out on the pier alone. Then, Renee and the family joined her, and they had a memorial service honoring Christy's fiancé. The family left the pier to give Christy some final time alone. Shortly thereafter, she threw her stone into the lake.

In the email, Renee said, "The sky was so unusual, I took some pictures of it."

I opened the first picture of the sky, and I thought it was pretty. Next, I opened the picture of Christy throwing the stone in the lake, and I cried.

Then, I opened the final picture of the sky after Christy threw the stone, and I gasped. I could hardly believe my eyes as I started praising God with my whole heart!

In the final picture of the *unusual* sky after Christy released the stone, the clouds formed the word "Shalom" in Hebrew letters. I confirmed what I saw with someone who knows Hebrew, and it was true. I asked Renee to tell her sister God was so pleased with what she did He wrote a special message for her in the sky!

Now...more of "the rest of the story."

Not too long afterwards, a man came into the store where Christy worked and, since her heart was open to love again, they began dating. They have been happily married for almost three years!

How about you? Is your heart prepared to receive the King? That's the real meaning of this season. Blessings await!

After Christmas--What?
Life Lesson #65

OUR FRIEND AND FELLOW PASTOR IN TEXAS HAS THE following saying, "There's nothing as over as Christmas." I know what Dan means. The gifts are opened. The work vacations are over. The decorations are down. The Christmas television shows no longer air. And the radio returns to regular programming instead of Christmas music.

I remember when people waited until after Thanksgiving to prepare for Christmas. Now, stores advertise and decorate for Christmas before Halloween. With such a long time to prepare and look forward to Christmas, it can seem like a real letdown when it is over. So I ask you the question, "After Christmas--what?"

I believe the answer to this question can be found in the lives of the characters surrounding the birth of Christ in the various biblical accounts. I hope looking at the question in this way will help us find the answers we need for our own lives. How about you? How about me? "After Christmas--what?"

First of all, I think it is very important for us to realize what Christmas really means. The celebration has become so intertwined with Santa Claus, reindeer, gift-giving, and love stories we sometimes forget what it's all about. Christmas, simply put, is "Emmanuel: God with us!" Christmas (even though the date was probably not December 25th) celebrates when *The Word became flesh and dwelt among us* (John 1:14). Jesus' birth was the greatest gift ever given to the world, and it's a gift offered to all who will receive Him.

So how did the biblical characters respond to God's greatest gift?

Mary Pondered.
But Mary treasured up all these things and pondered them in her heart (Luke 2:19).

Once we receive Jesus as our savior, it is very important for us to take time to *ponder* who He is and what this Gift means to us.

Personally, I like *to ponder* Jesus in the mornings when I first arise. I usually get a cup of what Patsy Clairmont calls "amber warmth" (hot tea), and sit for a few moments as I think about how wonderful He is. It's a special part of my day. Later I do Bible study, but I find this quiet time helps set the tone for the rest of the day. I'm amazed at what He reveals to me when I take time to ponder who He is.

Joseph followed God's guidance.

When they [the wise men] *had gone, an angel of the Lord appeared to Joseph in a dream. 'Get up,' he said, 'take the child and his mother and escape to Egypt. Stay there until I tell you for Herod is going to search for the child to kill him'* (Matthew 2:13). Once we receive Jesus, God's Holy Spirit indwells our hearts. Jesus said the Holy Spirit will *teach you everything and will remind you of everything I have told you* (John 14:26).

The Holy Spirit leads us in the ways God wants us to go. Joseph's obedience to God's guidance saved the life of his family. Your obedience to God's leading will fill your life with meaning.

The shepherds returned to work praising God.

The shepherds returned, glorifying and praising God for all the things they had heard and seen, which were just as they had been told (Luke 2:20).

It should be evident to the people with whom we work we've accepted Jesus, God's greatest gift. If our lives truly praise God, those around us will notice something different about us. I've heard time and again of how the atmosphere in an office or a factory changed because of one Christian on the work force.

When the days get hum-drum, and the work gets tedious, praising God can change our occupation from a job to a joy. Being a shepherd had its ups and downs, but the shepherds who encountered Jesus returned to their daily work praising God. Won't you join them?

The magi [wise men] presented him with gifts from their own treasures.

...Then they opened their treasures and presented him with gifts of gold, frankincense and myrrh (Matthew 2:11).

Once we truly receive the gift of salvation offered through Jesus, we desire to present our gifts to Him. But what could we possibly offer the King of Kings and Lord of Lords, the God of the Universe?

The gift He desires from us is not a tangible gift as those presented by the Magi. Instead, it is a gift from the heart. Obedience is the most precious gift we can give to God: *Does the Lord delight in burnt offerings and sacrifices as much as in obeying the Lord? To obey is better than sacrifice* (I Samuel 15:22).

Pondering God's attributes, obeying His leading, praising Him in our work place and daily living, and presenting Him gifts from our hearts--we can see from the characters surrounding the nativity how our lives should be once we have come to Jesus.

"O, Come Let Us Adore Him, Christ the Lord!"

Just Do It
Life Lesson #66

Don't put it off: do it now! Don't rest until you do
(Proverbs 6:4 NLT).

As we begin a new year full of fresh possibili-
ties, I hope this Life Lesson will motivate you. I must admit, it's one I have
to keep re-learning at different times in my life.

As strange as it may sound, I sometimes enjoy looking at commercials
on television and rating them as to how innovative or effective I think they
are. Some are brilliant and catch my attention immediately. Others, I feel,
are an insult to the viewer's intelligence.

As companies brand their products, they try to catch the essence of their
commodity in a slogan or tagline. Just for fun, I am going to give you some
taglines used through the years to see if you can remember which products
they represent. (I'll give you the answers at the end.)

1. "Breakfast of Champions"
2. "Mmm! Mmm! Good!"
3. "Can you hear me now?"
4. "Betcha can't eat just one!"
5. "Snap! Crackle! Pop!"
6. "Finger Lickin' Good"
7. "Melts in your mouth, not in your hand!"
8. "Where's the beef?"
9. "Good to the last drop!"
10. "Eat fresh!"

My personal favorite is the Nike tagline, "Just Do It." I cannot tell you
how many times I've repeated Nike's tagline when I was tempted to procrastinate. This new year is a blank slate. I pray I won't put off the things I
should do in the coming year. I hope I will *just do it*.

Before we look a little further at this phrase, let's consider a few of the
things that cause us to procrastinate in the first place.

1. Dread: We tend to delay doing things we do not like to do and/or fear doing.
2. Lack of clarity: We either don't know why we are doing what we're doing, or we don't know how it should be done.
3. Busy-ness: Sometimes I allow myself to become so busy I don't properly prioritize, so I just put everything off.
4. Habit: Each time we procrastinate it becomes easier to procrastinate the next time. Before long it becomes a habit. (But remember: habits can be broken.)

I feel the three short words in the brilliant Nike tagline, *Just Do It* contain valuable lessons for us on how to overcome procrastination. Let's consider them as a motivation for what could be the happiest and most productive new year of our lives.

Just-
Even though the word "just" as a noun usually carries the connotation of "fairness," as an adverb, it also can mean "now" ('immediately, at this moment, right now, straight away') or "simply" ('really, truly, definitely, absolutely.') In other words, if there's something you need to do, "simply do it now."

Do-
The word "do" means to "perform" ("accomplish, act, complete, achieve, carry out, get something done.")

Several years ago, I read about an experiment in which the CEO of a company had his employees write a list at the end of their work day of the things they needed to accomplish the following work day. The results were amazing, and the productivity increased astronomically.

I personally find if I follow that simple practice of setting goals, I am able to accomplish much more than if I don't. Without the list, I seem to flounder. Also, perhaps it's just my personality type, but getting to place a checkmark beside the things I complete on the list serves as a reward to me and makes me happy.

It-
"It" will be different for different people. This word is one of the most crucial words in the tagline.

It, among other definitions, means "the thing." What is "the thing" *you* need to "just do?" We often walk around feeling guilty for the things we do not do, and perhaps God did not intend for us to do them in the first place.

Life Lesson #20 was entitled, "Just Say No." In it we saw even Jesus did not do everything people asked Him to do. He often retreated alone to pray and seek what His priorities should be. Then He said "yes" to the things He was supposed to do and "no" to the others.

Let's make this new year a time to seek and to follow God's will. It may mean laying aside activities that have kept us too busy to do the things we should have been doing.

Once we do find what God desires for us to do, let's do it gladly, whole-heartedly, and promptly: *Whatever you do, work at it with all your heart, as working for the Lord*...(Colossians 3:23).

Are you ready to *Just Do It*? Now is the time.

Answers to the taglines:

1. Wheaties
2. Campbell Soup
3. Verizon
4. Lay's Potato Chips
5. Rice Krispies
6. Kentucky Fried Chicken
7. M & M's
8. Wendy's
9. Maxwell House Coffee
10. Subway

Things I've Learned from Our Grandchildren
Life Lesson #67

But Jesus said, 'Suffer little children, and forbid them not, to come unto me: for of such is the kingdom of heaven' (Matthew 19:14 KJV).

THIS VERSE PROMPTS A FUNNY MEMORY FROM YEARS ago. My friend, Norma, and I had nursery duty at church one Sunday night while the congregation was viewing a Christian movie. We had a room full of children of various ages and ran out of our planned activities. So, we decided to give them *free play* time.

As the service ran longer, and the children got wilder, I looked at Norma and asked, "When Jesus said, 'Suffer the little children to come unto me,' do you think He had ever kept a church nursery for this long?"

In her exhaustion, she immediately said, "I don't know, but He sure used the right word when He said, 'Suffer.'"

I still laugh about her response, but today I'd like to focus on the last part of that verse, '*...for of such is the kingdom of heaven.'* The kingdom of heaven is a rich study, and one we do not have room to address in this Life Lesson. In reference to children, I believe one meaning of this verse is children see the world more closely to the way God intends us to view it than we as adults do.

Some of the greatest Life Lessons I've learned have been through our grandchildren. The following are but a few of the things they've taught me:

1. **Love comes in various forms.**
   Life Lesson #61 was about love, and in it we saw the Greeks had four main categories for love: Eros--romantic love, Storge'--familial love, Phileo--friendship love, and Agape'-unconditional love.

   I suppose the love for grandchildren could come under the heading of Storge'--familial love, but I believe there should be a whole different word and category for the love you feel for grandchildren.

We have three grandchildren on earth, and two in heaven we will meet one day. At the time of this writing, our firstborn, Ty, is 10; our granddaughter, Mazi Grace, is 10 (they were born six weeks apart); and "the littlest one," Bronson, is 8.

In my lessons, I've tried not to bore you with endless details about them, but believe me, I could have! The love I feel for them is so deep, so real, so true it's hard to even describe. Grandchildren truly do bring a whole new meaning to the word, "love."

2. **It's fun to giggle and laugh.**
   I told someone recently I think this was the best Christmas of my life. After I said those words, I wondered what made it so, and I realized it was the grandchildren.

We had a week-long pajama party, and our house was filled with giggles and laughter the whole time. Their giggles would immediately prompt smiles on the faces of the adults.

In a book I wrote several years ago, I included the following facts:

Babies begin to laugh around ten weeks of age.
About six weeks later, they are laughing once each hour.
By the age of four years, they are laughing once every four minutes.
The average adult in America only laughs about fifteen times a day.
(Some researchers say as little as four times a day.)

The older we get, the more we understand God's goodness, so why are we less happy?

Let's at least be willing to return to days of grins, giggles, laughter and happiness. After all, as the saying goes, "Life is too important to be taken too seriously." (An unnamed newspaper editor based this statement on a quote by Oscar Wilde.)

3. **Don't hold grudges.**
   One minute the children cuddled up on the couch and played games on the iPad. The next, they created sets for their original play. The next they set up a hot chocolate stand in the yard.

   Then, it would happen. One would lament the other did "so and so," followed by a few minutes of pouting. But almost before I could turn around, it was over, done, and they were the Three Musketeers again.

   They seem to realize holding grudges only wastes their play time. While they are pouting, the others are still having fun.

Oh, if we as adults could learn that valuable lesson! So many people sit on the sidelines licking their wounds, and the game goes on without them.

I could keep going when it comes to talking about what "my babies" have taught me, but I'll close with one final thought. They seem to be able to enjoy life to the fullest because they trust their parents to take care of the serious stuff in their lives.

Can we learn to enjoy life to the fullest knowing our Heavenly Father will take care of the serious stuff in our lives? It's true!

OUT OF THE BLUE
LIFE LESSON #68

I foretold the former things long ago, my mouth announced them and I made them known; then SUDDENLY I acted, and they came to pass (Isaiah 48:3).

WE LEFT A GROWING, BUSTLING CHURCH TO ACCEPT God's very specific call to a little church in New Jersey. It was a wonderful experience, and some close friendships were made during our four years there.

We were planning a children's Christmas musical, "Hark, the Herald Angel." I decided to hang blue cloth from ceiling to floor in the choir loft to represent heaven and let the children help put cotton clouds on it.

However, all the material I could find in our area of New Jersey was very expensive. A friend in our former church was the head of a cloth finishing company in my hometown in South Carolina, and I called him to see if we could buy some sky blue material at a discounted rate. He was not in his office, so I left a message asking him to return my call.

Shortly thereafter, he called me back. After we chatted a few minutes, I told him why I had called. "Warren, do you have any sky blue material I could buy at a discounted rate for our church here in New Jersey?"

Silence. At first, I thought we might have gotten disconnected. "Warren, are you still there?"

An almost shaky voice replied, "Joy, the reason I was not in my office when you called is because I was in the warehouse looking at inventory."

He explained there were two round bolts of sky blue material standing alone in the corner, and he asked the manager about their purpose. The manager replied they had no idea, and they were not even sure how the cloth got there. Warren told him to dispose of it.

Then, Warren immediately walked into his office and returned my call. I asked him for sky blue material.

"You can not only have it," he said, "I'll even pay the shipping for you!" God answered that request *out of the blue* literally.

The phrase, "out of the blue," is an English idiom that comes from the old saying, "a bolt from the blue." A bolt refers to a lightning bolt, and the blue refers to the blue sky. Just as it is unusual for a thunderstorm to strike

160

when the sky is blue, anything that happens suddenly or unexpectedly is considered *out of the blue*.

One of the Life Lessons I've learned is what appears to be *out of the blue* for us is already known by God. Let's look at some things that happened *out of the blue* in scripture and what we can learn from them.

1. **Things may seem to happen *out of the blue*, but timing is one of God's greatest miracles.**
   ...the LORD drove the sea back with a strong east wind and turned it into dry land. The waters were divided (Exodus 14:21).

   The parting of the Red Sea is remarkable miracle. But to me, a miracle just as great, is God parted the sea at the exact time it was needed! When things come *out of the* blue, remember they did not surprise God.

2. **An *out of the blue* experience gives us power for every day living.**
   Suddenly there was a great earthquake! For an angel of the Lord came down from heaven, rolled aside the stone, and sat on it (Matthew 28:2 NLT).

   The same power that brought Jesus out of the grave indwells each believer. The Greek word for "power" is *dunamis*, and it is the root word for "dynamite." Through Jesus we have the power—the dynamite—to live in victory and not succumb to defeat. The choice is ours.

3. **God often accomplishes His purposes through *out of the blue* experiences.**
   ...suddenly a bright light from heaven flashed around me. I fell to the ground and heard a voice say to me, 'Saul! Saul! Why do you persecute me?' 'Who are you, Lord?' I asked (Acts 22:6-7).

   Paul (Saul) was blinded on the Damascus Road after this encounter with the risen Christ. Ananias healed him. Ananias then said God had chosen Paul for the Damascus Road experience so he could tell all the world he had seen the Righteous One and heard His voice. As we know, Paul's witness spread the gospel and expanded the church exponentially.

4. **Prayer and praise precede *out of the blue* experiences.**
   Suddenly there was such a violent earthquake that the foundations of the prison were shaken. At once all the prison doors flew open, and everyone's chains came loose (Acts 16: 26).

   Paul and Silas were in prison praying and praising God at midnight when they were set free by an *out of the blue* earthquake.

Some of you may be thinking, "But my *out of the blue* experiences have not been good." Always remember scripture tells us, and our past experiences prove: *in all things God works for the good of those who love him...* (Romans 8:28).

Let's live in resurrection power, pray often, praise God continually, and look for the ways God will work in our lives *out of the blue*!

Heaven
Life Lesson #69

But as it is written: 'Eye has not seen, nor ear heard, nor have entered into the heart of man the things God has prepared for those who love Him.' But God has revealed them to us through His Spirit. For the Spirit searches all things, yes, the deep things of God (I Corinthians 2:9-10 NKJV).

I PLANNED TO WRITE A LIFE LESSON ON HEAVEN THE next to the last Life Lesson in this series. Little did I realize I would be writing it today--five years from the day my mother died. So this subject is especially dear to me right now.

One of the things I've tried to do with the Life Lessons is to be transparent. With that in mind, I don't want you to think I'm being heretical with some of the things I will share. I'm just trying to be honest with my feelings.

Through most of my life, I didn't think about heaven much, even though I knew through Jesus heaven would be my eternal home. I believe the reason I didn't dwell my thoughts on heaven is because I had a hard time relating to it. I was taught heaven was not like the earth. It was an ethereal existence of disembodied spirits floating around. Somewhere along the line, images of angels (most of them short and chubby) sitting on clouds playing harps entered into the scene of heaven.

Although we would be with many people we knew, I wasn't sure what all we would do. I knew we would be in God's presence, and we would continuously worship Him.

We would be free from bad things like sickness and pain. I knew heaven would be beautiful with pearly gates and streets of gold, but I felt I would miss the things I love here on earth. I am embarrassed to admit this, but from what I understood of heaven, it did not seem exciting to me.

In recent years, through reading Randy Alcorn's book <u>Heaven</u>, I realize most of the teaching on heaven is based on the thinking of Greek philosophers rather than on the Bible. Plato was especially influential in today's concept of heaven.

The Greeks of his day believed the spiritual was good and the physical (even the body) was bad. So heaven could not include anything the physical would desire. Thus the idea of disembodied spirits filling heaven took root.

However, the Greek philosophers missed the all-important biblical concept of how God views the world. He sees our world in cycles of time—the perfect world He created, the fallen world (in which we live), and the new heaven and the new earth (the eternal heaven.)

The Bible talks frequently about the new heaven and the new earth. In Genesis, God dwelled in heaven, but He chose to come to earth to commune with Adam and Eve. With the new heaven, God's dwelling place comes to a perfected earth. Amazing!

Just reading Revelation 21-22 should fill us with excitement to see what we will experience in the eternal heaven. We will receive a new body and a new mind as we're restored to perfection. Sin will be gone forever. Sickness, pain, suffering, and death are removed.

Plants and trees, rivers, the sea, lush vegetation will abound. We will operate in the fruit of the Spirit and the strengths of our spiritual gifts. We will learn and create with a pure heart. Animals and people will live in harmony.

We will enjoy fellowship with each other, rejoice together, and enjoy delicious foods (i.e. the marriage supper of the Lamb.)

Finally, and most importantly, we will celebrate God's goodness, and His glory will be shown in all things. Heaven will be wonderful, and it will be a far cry from disembodied spirits floating around.

However, the Bible is clear--only one entrance exists to this wonderful place. Through Jesus' atoning sacrifice, our names must be written in the Lamb's Book of Life (Revelation 21:27).

Alcorn relates the following story: Professional singer, Ruthanna Metzgar, sang at the wedding of a very wealthy man in Seattle. Afterwards, she and her husband, Roy, arrived at the lavish reception. The bride and groom approached a beautiful glass and brass staircase that led to the top floor. Someone cut the satin ribbon across the bottom of the staircase to allow the bride and groom to go up the stairs followed by their guests.

When Ruthanna and Roy arrived at the top of the stairs, a maître d' with a bound book greeted the guests. They gave their names. He searched and told them he could not find their names. He searched again.

When their names were not found, Ruthanna explained she had sung at the wedding. The maître d' replied, "I don't care who you are or what you did. Without your name in the book you cannot attend the banquet."

The couple was escorted to a service elevator where they were told to leave. You see, in the busy-ness of preparing to sing for the wedding, Ruthanna failed to reply to the invitation.

Have you accepted Christ's invitation? It's open to all who will respond! And, oh, the joys that await us in heaven!

"Finding Joy"
Life Lesson #70

'I have told you this so that my joy may be in you and that your joy may be complete' (John 15:11).

As I complete this series of Life Lessons, I want to end with one I hope will encourage you and assist you in the quest for living life to its fullest. I believe we all are on a journey trying to find joy even while living in a world that often robs us of it. All of the 70 Life Lessons in this series culminate with these practical suggestions for "Finding Joy" today, tomorrow, and always!

- **Learn to adapt to life's changes.**
  When Wayne performs a wedding, he uses a phrase I love at the end of the marriage vows--"through all the changing scenes of life." Life does change. The couple standing before him will experience mountains and valleys together, and life fifty years from that day will look different to them than it does at that moment.

  I've heard it said the only sure thing in life is change. Life events and circumstances change; people change; we change. Change is not always bad. Some changes are necessary in order to move us out of a rut of complacency. Change requires adapting our skills and even our interests to find contentment and joy in our different "scenes of life."

  The Serenity Prayer beautifully expresses what our response to change should be: "God, grant me the serenity to accept the things I cannot change, courage to change the things I can, and wisdom to know the difference." (Reinhold Niebuhr, American theologian.)

Change what we can to make life better. Accept what we cannot change.

- **Put our trust in the Unchangeable One.**
  Life changes; people change; we change. However, God never changes!
  Jesus Christ is the same yesterday and today and forever (Hebrews 13:8).
  Every good and perfect gift is from above, coming down from the Father of the heavenly lights, who does not change like shifting shadows (James 1:17).

  What are some of God's characteristics that do not change? God is Love. God is Light. God is Truth. God, in ways we may not always see, works to make good come from the changes in our lives (Romans 8:28).

  So no matter what we are facing, we can hold on to God, for only He is steadfast and unchanging.

- **Why worry when we can pray?**
  My mother-in-law had a plaque in her kitchen window that said, "Why worry when you can pray?" It was such a simple, yet profound, reminder God is in control.

  One reason people doubt the validity of that statement is we often enter into prayer with preconceived ideas of what we think should happen as a result of our prayers. If things don't happen the way we feel they should, we begin to doubt the importance of prayer, or even the sovereignty of God.

Scripture tells us: *Do not be anxious about anything, but in every situation, by prayer and petition, with thanksgiving, present your requests to God* (Philippians 4:6).

This verse shows we can trust God (*do not be anxious about anything*), we should come before God with thankful hearts (*with thanksgiving*), and God hears our prayers (*present your requests to God.*)

Prayer is much more than a wish list we offer to God. It is a chance to acknowledge our faith in and thankfulness to the Unchangeable One who works for good in all situations. Worry is one of the biggest joy-robbers in life. Trust is one of the greatest joy-builders in life.

- **Joy multiplies when we share it.**
  I call it, "God's mathematics." The more joy we share with others the more joy we receive. Sometimes, all a person needs are an encouraging word and a listening ear. We can't make another person happy or joyful, but we can look for ways to foster an atmosphere and/or an attitude of joy.

One day I stopped to have lunch at a little mountain restaurant. The server was very curt and borderline rude to us as customers. When she brought my food, I asked if she had any prayer concerns I could pray for her when I thanked God for the food. She quickly said, "No, thank you, I'm fine." I told her I would include a "thank you" to God that she was fine.

A few minutes later she came back to my table, pulled up a chair, and sat down. She told me her aunt who had raised her was dying, and tears filled her eyes. As I listened, I could tell she hurt deeply, and I assured her of my prayers. She got up from my table and made the rounds to her other customers, but her whole attitude had changed.

Even the customers looked at each other as though wondering what had happened. Sometimes just letting people know we care is all it takes to help them find joy.

"Finding Joy" is a lifelong process, and the answer is not found at the end of the rainbow, but in the daily journey of life when we choose joy in whatever circumstances we face. It's a choice we will never regret.

Thank you, as the reader, for joining me on this journey of a lifetime—literally (at least up until now.) I pray you find your joy through the true Joy-Giver, Jesus Christ! I love you!

How to Become a Christian--a Follower of Jesus Christ

THROUGHOUT THE LIFE LESSONS IN THIS BOOK YOU have read: *True joy comes through a relationship with Jesus Christ.* Some people do not accept Christ, and others may doubt their salvation, because they fear they do not know the *right* things to do to become a Christian. Sadly, others wilfully reject the decision to follow Jesus.

Becoming a Christian, a follower of Jesus Christ, simply put is a heart-change, and it is unique to each person.

The heart-change comes through the realization of the following scriptural principles:

- **Each person is a sinner.**
  All have sinned and come short of the glory of God (Romans 3:23).
  Sin is "missing the mark" of God's standards which He put in place for our good.

- **God is holy and just, so therefore He must punish sin.**
  For the wages of sin is death (Romans 6:23a).

- **God loves us so much He took the punishment for our sins. That's called "grace."**
  But, God demonstrated His own love for us in this: While we were still sinners, Christ died for us (Romans 5:8).

- **We cannot earn such love. It is a gift freely given by God.**
  But the gift of God is eternal life in Christ Jesus our Lord (Romans 6:23b).

- **We must recognize only God can change our sinful hearts.**

> *For it is by grace you have been saved, through faith—and this is not from yourselves, it is the gift of God—not by works, so that no one can boast* (Ephesians 2:8,9).

- **The heart-change occurs when we admit our sinful condition, ask God for forgiveness, and accept the gift of His great love.**
  If we confess our sins, he is faithful and just and will forgive us our sins and purify us from all unrighteousness (I John 1:9).

- **When we accept God's gift, we become children of God and part of His family.**
  Yet to all who did receive him, to those who believed in his name, he gave the right to become children of God (John 1:12).

If you positively responded to the above, you accept by faith that you are now a Christian. You may or may not feel differently right away, but you will find that you love Jesus and desire to show His love to others. It is important to consistently read the Bible, pray, and fellowship with other believers so you can grow to be more like Jesus. May God bless you! You have found your Joy!

ACKNOWLEDGMENTS

I WANT TO EXPRESS A VERY SPECIAL THANK YOU TO Rodger Painter who designed the front book cover. I appreciate his work, I appreciate his friendship, but most of all, I appreciate his heart for God!

You will see the names of my family members in the Life Lessons quite a bit: my soul-mate and best-friend husband, Wayne (who proofread the Life Lessons before I posted them), our precious daughters, Meri Beth (husband, Thomas, and son, Ty), and Molly (husband, Christman, and children, Mazi Grace and Bronson), and my multi-talented sister, Lynn. Their love and support not only for this project, but also in life, bring daily doses of joy to my heart.

In looking back, I realize many of the most significant Life Lessons I've learned have been through the way they live and love, and I thank them. I also cherish the memories of things I learned through my parents, James and Jeri Clary, who are now experiencing the fullness of joy in God's presence. Each--and all--are a major part of this book.

ABOUT THE AUTHOR

JOY CLARY BROWN IS AN INSPIRATIONAL AUTHOR and speaker. She has written, co-written, or been a contributing writer in twelve books and has traveled extensively speaking to both Christian and secular groups. Joy's messages, whether written or spoken, are insightful and encouraging. She is known for correlating New Testament scriptures with their Hebrew context, yet keeping the messages practical, applicable, and fun. Joy also writes and speaks on biblical health and nutrition.

Joy and her husband, Wayne, founded *Diversified Ministries* as a way to help spread the gospel locally, nationally, and globally. She is the mother of two daughters, Meri Beth (married to Thomas Howard) and Molly (married to Christman Howard), and the happy grandmother of her three "little loves," Ty, Mazi Grace, and Bronson.

Joy desires to see people come into a relationship with Jesus Christ and to grow in joyful fellowship with Him.

For further information, Joy can be contacted at www.wordsofjoy.org

About the Photographer

Rodger Painter is a freelance writer, photographer, and motion picture cameraman. He worked for many years as a staff writer, photographer, and editor in newspaper. His work earned more than a dozen awards in news, feature writing, and photography in competitions sponsored by the South Carolina Press Association, the National Newspaper Association, and the National Newspaper Editorial Workshop.

Rodger also worked for years in the motion picture industry as a still photographer and cameraman on more than three dozen feature films, numerous TV commercials, made-for-TV movies, and documentaries. His work has taken him from coast to coast across the USA and south of the equator.

Having grown up at Cape Canaveral, Florida, the home of many rocket launches and NASA space missions, Rodger has a strong interest in science, particularly space science and rocketry. He was among the participants in NASA's Journalist in Space program.

Currently, he and his wife, Elaine, reside in upstate South Carolina. They have two children and two grandchildren.